THE

LEAP

YEARS

To Barbara — best wishes in the leap years to come. I hope to meet you someday (even if you do look 29!)

Best wishes — Nutei

WOMEN

REFLECT ON CHANGE,

LOSS, AND

LOVE

The Leap Years

EDITED BY

MARY ANNE MAIER AND

JOAN SHADDOX ISOM

BEACON PRESS

BOSTON

Beacon Press
25 Beacon Street
Boston, Massachusetts 02108-2892
www.beacon.org

Beacon Press books
are published under the auspices of
the Unitarian Universalist Association of Congregations.

05 04 03 02 01 00   8 7 6 5 4 3 2

Text design by Margaret M. Wagner
Composition by Wilsted & Taylor Publishing Services

Library of Congress Cataloging-in-Publication Data

The leap years : women reflect on change, loss, and love / edited by
    Mary Anne Maier and Joan Shaddox Isom.
        p.   cm.
    ISBN 0-8070-6515-3 (pa. : acid-free paper)
    1. Women.   2. Change.   3. Loss (Psychology).   4. Love.   I. Maier,
    Mary Anne.   II. Isom, Joan Shaddox.
    HQ1111.L43   1999
    305.4—dc21   99-27395

In memory of

DOROTHY SHADDOX CUTHBERTSON,
who brought light and life into every room she entered

and

HELEN KELLEY MAIER,
*who knew more about beginnings and endings
than she ever let on.*

CONTENTS

INTRODUCTION

THE MOTHER TONGUE . . . [IS] COMMON, COMMON SPEECH, COLLOQUIAL, LOW, ORDINARY, PLEBEIAN, LIKE THE WORK ORDINARY PEOPLE DO, THE LIVES COMMON PEOPLE LIVE. THE MOTHER TONGUE, SPOKEN OR WRITTEN, EXPECTS AN ANSWER. IT IS CONVERSATION, A WORD THE ROOT OF WHICH MEANS "TURNING TOGETHER." THE MOTHER TONGUE IS LANGUAGE NOT AS MERE COMMUNICATION BUT AS RELATION, RELATIONSHIP. IT CONNECTS. IT GOES TWO WAYS, MANY WAYS, AN EXCHANGE, A NETWORK. ITS POWER IS NOT IN DIVIDING BUT IN BINDING, NOT IN DISTANCING BUT IN UNITING. IT IS WRITTEN, BUT NOT BY SCRIBES AND SECRETARIES FOR POSTERITY; IT FLIES FROM THE MOUTH ON THE BREATH THAT IS OUR LIFE AND IS GONE, LIKE THE OUTBREATH, UTTERLY GONE AND YET RETURNING, REPEATED, THE BREATH THE SAME AGAIN ALWAYS, EVERYWHERE, AND WE ALL KNOW IT BY HEART.
—*Ursula K. Le Guin*
"Bryn Mawr Commencement Address (1986)"

When we set out to create this anthology, we wanted above all to discover and share authentic voices. We hoped that, given a suitable catalyst, most people would jump at the chance to experience the exchange, the connection, the relationship that comes from sharing true stories, the stories that tell us who we are. We've always known that authentic stories belong as much to the listener, or reader, as to the teller, or writer, because such stories go "two ways, many ways, an exchange, a network." And so we believed that by bringing together writers and readers in this holy communication, we could spark countless unifying conversations, not only among individuals but *within* them.

Inviting the participants to this conversation demanded some difficult decisions. Both of us feel strongly that such vital discourse should never be limited to one group, even if that group is itself half the human race, as women are. And yet women, who have, until relatively recently, been excluded from the conversation that is accepted literature, are the ones left speaking among themselves in the natural language, the authentic language of their lives. "It's often easier for women to trust one another," Le Guin points out, "to try to speak our experience in our own language, the language we talk to each other in, the mother tongue; so we empower one another." This is the language we were seeking, so we chose to invite women to be the writers in this conversation. We certainly hope men will join the conversation as readers, for surely these stories that speak women's experience in women's language will resonate for them, just as much of the literature written by men has affected women over the centuries. Perhaps this collection will serve as a small offering toward an ongoing conversation of our shared humanity.

Some define a proper anthology as a collection of pre-published pieces by high-profile authors, all containing roughly the same level of writing—of formality, diction, and syntax. Many excellent anthologies of this type exist. But we agreed from the start that we had to step outside that framework if we were to create the anthology we imagined. Millions of women who don't speak the language of power might believe that because their voices are never heard, they don't exist. But we knew in our hearts that so many women, ordinary women, had important stories to tell and authentic voices with which to tell them. So we invited these ordinary women to share stories from their own lives. As we read the hundreds of wondrously varied and powerful essays that poured in, we discovered one vital flaw in our thinking: None of these women is ordinary. Is there such a thing? We no longer think so.

We chose to include a few well-established writers, known for the clarity and honesty of their writing, side by side with the emerging writers represented here, deciding it was a compliment to each to be invited into the good company of the other. The faithful readers of writers such as Margaret Atwood, Diane Ackerman, Gloria Wade-Gayles,

Maxine Kumin, Diane Glancy, and Madeleine L'Engle can anticipate the always-beautiful language of lucidity and simplicity offered here by their favorites.

Before we could invite any of these contributors, we first had to determine what catalyst might inspire the conversations we had in mind, the telling of stories, of truths, that we all know by heart. We hoped the broad, frightening, perpetual yet heart-stoppingly specific topic of *transition* might do the trick. Change is something that a few of us anticipate eagerly, most fear, and none can elude. We are all shaped by change—sometimes strengthened, other times merely hardened; sometimes diminished, other times blessedly softened. Those crystallized instants of transition (which might take years to unfold, decades to fathom), whether agonizing or enthralling, are often the moments in which we feel ourselves most alive. As the mounds of manuscripts grew each day in response to our single call for essays about change, about transformation, we knew we'd found the catalyst.

We worked through the months amidst bales of manuscripts, reading each one carefully (sometimes aloud to each other), reading some four and five and six times apiece. It was during this process that we learned we weren't alone in our desire to share the stories that make us who we are. "Let me know about this anthology," one woman wrote in a cover letter. "I want to know how I can get a copy, even if you don't publish my story." And over and over again we read words to this effect: "Thank you for encouraging me to tell my story; I'm so glad to finally look at it myself." We're firm believers that much of writing is, and rightly should be, talking to ourselves in order to make sense of things, so we were pleased that a simple nudge could excite our contributors' desires for setting off on such important journeys within, for joining us in telling our own truths.

What erupted from this spark we set was an abundance of humor and heartache, of the extraordinary and the everyday. Women shared their deepest experiences of joy and pain and uncertainty, of loving and learning, of loss and hope. We had no ideology to advance, no cause to promote with this collection but one: Every woman has a story to tell. Submissions came from around the country and some from around the world; from a few who approached telling their own stories as a whim and many who seemed almost desperate to do so; from young women of fourteen and women rejoicing in their eighties; from women of various cultures and ethnicities; from lesbians and heterosexuals—single, married, and divorced; from the abused, the lost, the amused and triumphant. The women who finally became a part of this collection create an abundance for all of us with the sharing of their rich insights and resonant uncertainties.

The variety of these essays is astounding, yet their unity remains at the deepest level, in the mother tongue: "language not as mere communication but as relation, relationship." Thus one woman approaches romantic love by letting us in on her consuming crush on a much younger man, while another shares love letters unfolding the delicate bloom of the greatest love she's ever known, a love she discovers at midlife with another woman. Still another offers the funny-sad tale of pushing away a husband she only thought she didn't love: "If he could only be richer, thicker, smarter, and slicker, I used to think, I'd be happy."

Some women seem to celebrate the common nature of their experiences, while others feel utterly alone in theirs. In "Moodswings and Midlife," for example, Elayne Clift takes us through the foibles and very real fears that women must face with menopause and beyond. Yet "when those dark moments seem more than I can possibly sort out," Clift tells us, "I try to remind myself that I am in the best of company." Diane Ackerman, on the other hand, shares the secret of her own survival as a child, when her deep aloneness led her to create the powerful and saving fantasy of belonging to a group of extraterrestrial itinerant artists who traveled the universe learning the art forms of various beings and thus their profoundest feelings and needs.

Humor is the rock undergirding several of the essays. Margaret Atwood's official version of how she became a poet calls forth chortles even as it dumps us off the high horse of Literature with a capital L:

> I was once a snub-nosed blonde. My name was Betty. I had a perky personality and was a cheerleader for the college football team. My favorite color was pink. Then I became a poet. My hair darkened overnight, my nose lengthened, I gave up football for the cello, my real name disappeared and was replaced by one that had a chance of being taken seriously, and my clothes changed color in the closet, all by themselves, from pink to black.

And other of these uncommon women invite us to laugh at other unlikely subjects. In "Jukebox Lazarus," Rhonda C. Poynter tells us how difficult it can be to believe your father is really dead—especially when he's been dying every few months for as long as you can remember as his way of staying one state line ahead of the bill collectors. Of course we can't help but ache for Poynter at the same time that she shares with a wink her early understanding of the flimflam game and her role as the bereaved mourner: "If I could bring up the hiccups and trembling, I'd get a ten-dollar bill or more out of the performance for myself. I'd be sitting down at the 7-Eleven with a fistful of candy bars and a movie magazine by the time the mark got home."

We come at life's changes in different ways, and we leave them as different people. There's no road map, no guidebook, and certainly no appropriate or inevitable or even predictable reaction to our own transformations. In her collection of Native American women writers called *Spider Woman's Granddaughters*, Laguna Pueblo-Sioux author Paula Gunn Allen makes a powerful observation: "Sometimes transformation occurs as a consequence of victory, but as often it occurs as a consequence of defeat."

Sometimes we inch our way through a change, sifting every detail again and again until we're left with an essential kernel, an understanding, or perhaps only a regret. We find such gleanings in Jane Brox's "The Early Land," where we can discern with her the slightest difference in sound between her brother's first spring plowing and her father's—a difference telling the story, in its tranquil way, of her largely altered life. Such quiet sifting occurs again in a very different essay, "Querida Nuria," in which author Joan Lindgren uses the epistolary form to share her heart with a Chilean woman whose powerful transformation from years of political imprisonment creates an inner peace strong enough to transform the author as well.

At other times we feel the need to trace the dips and curves of life that have led to a particular transition. Did these events in our history lead inevitably to this change or merely precede it? If we retrace our steps, might we discover who we are along the way? Such tracings unfold beautifully in Laura Distelheim's heart-grabbing "On Loving Ethan." Within a single paragraph Distelheim draws us into the nursery and into her heart as she consciously decides not to love her five-month-old nephew, just diagnosed with a life-threatening illness. We hold our breaths with Distelheim as she retraces the rough terrain of this journey, and in the end we understand that only love could have pulled her through it all.

Then there are the straight-out transformations, those life changes that leave us wondering who in the world we were *before*, and how there could be such an absolute line forever separating *then* from *now*. But there it is: the line in the sand we may not have known existed, let alone imagined we'd cross one day. Gloria Wade-Gayles reveals with painstaking honesty the horror and self-doubt that became a part of her life literally overnight after a terrifying personal attack and near rape. "Like battered women," Wade-Gayles tells us, "victims of rape or attempted rape drink an acid mixture of pain and guilt." Yet her eyes are opened by this attack not only to fear but to love and understanding as she realizes the strength of her son and daughter's encompassing love for her, and the pain of her son and all young African American men who are etched "in national thinking as criminals who should be avoided, who should be feared." Such honest appraisal, such telling of truths, leads to transformation as well in Beth Kephart's "Sharing a Room." When technology fails her in the confines of a sterile hospital room, it is the woman in the next bed—the woman she thought could not be further from her in every aspect of life, the woman whom she had ardently wished out of her space —whose sense of common humanity saves Kephart in the end, reshaping forever the author's concept of otherness.

We close the collection with Susan Marsh's "Re-creation," in which she's staring into the apparent abyss awaiting her across that absolute line of transformation. "I am in the middle of a leap," Marsh says, putting into words the apprehensions and triumphs painted so vibrantly in all these essays. Marsh takes heart, finally, from the example of a brave little spider who rappels into the unknown on a fragile silk thread, an act that leaves the author yearning as so many of us do: "If only I could launch with such fearlessness and grace."

"Women . . . are discarding the masks," Gloria Norris proclaims in *The Seasons of Women*. She notes that women are feeling "sufficiently empowered now to see our own daily struggles as moral and dramatic theater worthy of sharing as a part of human revelation." We find the essays we've gathered here to be nothing short of revelation, leaving us feeling both honored and enriched by the privilege of entering these women's lives at moments that matter most to them.

After having her essay accepted for the collection, one contributor wrote us a wonderful long letter continuing the conversation begun in her essay. She closed by saying, "I know this has been a very unprofessional response letter, but the story is probably the most important one I have ever written . . . and it helped me to put a lot to rest."

Lots of things are put to rest in this collection. Lots of things are just beginning.

Some Bit of Love to Chew On

We wake, if we wake at all, to mystery.

—Annie Dillard

THE UNDERFED HUMAN HEART

ADRIAN BLEVINS

He left because I asked him to. Or because he knew I could not myself endure to do it. Or because underneath the pain he bore from feeling he'd long since lost me, there was somewhere within him the great dream of becoming his own man in untouched space—of calling the shots in a neighborhood of his own choosing while the sunlight cast down an unrestricted future from some unwomaned window. In any case, I had had my own such stupid fantasies, so what does it matter? We'd been folding up each other's T-shirts since before we were adults, and to tell you the truth, I used to leave the rooms he'd enter thinking of ways I might manage an unbonding without hurting either one of us or our boys, going so far one night as to ask the woman who would become his lover for information on how she'd managed to *kindly undo* what I now know cannot—and probably should not—kindly be undone.

I thought of our separation as though I were planning a little trip to Europe or he were going to spend a year hiking the Appalachian Trail. I began to think of it in the first place because I couldn't look at him without wishing he were other than he was: If he could only be richer, thicker, smarter, and slicker, I used to think, I'd be happy. I wanted him to own a Jeep. Or at least a house. I wanted him to command any room he walked into with a voice as deep as some African sea that didn't even exist; I wanted him to slam his fist upon the table and demand that I behave myself. I wanted him to look into my eyes and see the roaring, un-fixable, unspeakable phraseology of unhappiness, and then? I wanted him to *un*roar and fix and speak all that made me want another life. I wanted him to save me.

Perhaps I thought that his leaving would do it. Perhaps I thought that if I had to look at my life without him in it, I would be able to see all that I knew, somehow, was still there: how much I loved him when he sang *one for the money, two for the show* when he'd carry one of the boys to bed, how he made me laugh when he'd stand at the counter beside the stove and chop onions, then suddenly pick up the telephone and shout into it a complaint about the government, and how often I would think of him when we were off in our together-but-separate lives, hoping he'd come home at least by dinnertime for no other reason than because there was no place he'd rather be. Perhaps I thought that I'd see him clearly once he was gone, that missing him would give me empathy enough to see his life for what we'd together made it. Here was a man not even forty struggling with his own longings and choices in a world that would do its best to kick his legs right out from under him—an artist in a world that could not afford to value grace or light. Perhaps I hoped that in the aftermath of the leaving, I would be able to *feel* as well as think all that made my man my man.

And this is, in fact, what happened.

But by the time I'd cleared up the chaos between my un-realistic ideas and the everyday truths about a man who, like any other, was just as defined by nurturing hands that could knead bread as by a bad singing voice, he'd already met her.

As I have said in other places, women, if they are the least bit attuned to their own natures, have powers that are too subtle, too ancient, and too enmeshed in the biological surf of need to be spoken of in words other than those words that address mystery. A woman who's found what she wants—hair, skin, voice, thought, feeling, wrist, arm, shoulder—a woman who's found a man just standing there homeless and heartbroken and ready for the taking—ah, now here's a woman with whom you'll need to contend.

I used to get into intellectual discussions about how stupid it was for women to hate the other women their boyfriends and husbands ran off with. It just didn't seem logical to me: He was the one who'd done the betraying, if any betraying had been done; she'd just taken up with someone she liked. Why was she to blame? I even remember snickering a bit at a story a friend told me about beating up his wife's lover (who later claimed to have been attacked by a gang of furious men)—*why the man*, I remember asking. Why the *man*?

My friend had shrugged.

Now I understand that shrug, but I'm too embarrassed to elaborate on the details. I'll just skip all that: the ranting and the raving, the following him out to his car after he'd kept the children here while I'd taught, the ambiguous answers coming flat and black out of his mouth, the last kisses on the mouth and the hand, their trip to Memphis and the Nancy Drew way I found out about it. I'll just skip that phone call to Memphis. I'll even skip the part of the story where she had lunch with my sister and mother—the way she wept like a sick baby and talked about destiny and the meant-to-be. I'll skip what happened to her truck, too, though I will say that it happened at dusk with a tree stump and that a friend of mine told me I "looked good doing it." I'll even skip the catharsis—the feeling I had just minutes later when the world went blue. And the daily effects since: the clean house, the washed-off back porch, the new poems, this essay.

I constantly try to remind my students that one of the reasons it's important to read about the struggles of others is that we learn through such efforts how universal the human experience is. Sure, some of us don't take our frustrations out on trucks or have to contend with such things as the upcoming September wedding in which the three of us must show up prepared to bridesmaid and best man and speak in clothes that ought to stay on mannequins, but we all, one day or another, will have to experience either the difficulties of unbinding those sorts of bonds that couldn't make us happy or of choosing not to. And more of us than I'd like to know will also have to contend with the irrational parts of our own natures, behaving in unredeemable ways that finally unbind all that should have remained bound up and certain in the first place.

I admit to wishing that I were a wolf or one of those birds that mate for life. And I admit to wishing that I had not done many of the things I have done in the past few months—I admit to failing to understand the difference between thought and feeling. And the absurd regressions embarrass me, I'm telling you. But as costly as they were, I must also claim alliance to them, for they showed me—there in that wet and dusky summer evening when the world went blue and I realized that it was my *own self* I'd have to love and honor and never betray—that I do not lie—absolutely do not lie—when I tell my students how crazy is this thing we might as well call the underfed human heart.

ON LOVING ETHAN

LAURA S. DISTELHEIM

As soon as I heard the news, I decided not to love Ethan. He was five months old then, all velvet head and milky breath and dimpled fist around my finger, but I told myself I still had a chance to disengage his hold on my heart. I was at my sister's apartment with my parents that day, waiting for her and her husband to bring him back from the doctor, for them to come through the door with him swaying in his car seat, unzip his bunting, say, *phew*, what a scare; waiting for all of us to laugh and talk at once until he wailed for his bottle, then for us to laugh some more, watching his cheeks rise and fall, saying: Would you look at him go? How could we have even thought it? and: With an appetite like that he'll be a football player yet—when the phone rang.

It was later when I decided—when I was in the rocking chair in his nursery, listening again and again to the memory of my sister's sob, hearing how it had slipped from the phone in that last instant before we hung up, each of us in a different room, clutching receivers that had turned to fishhooks to pull us, thrashing and gasping, from the warm waters of Before into the alien air of From Now On. I was rocking back and forth, back and forth, holding onto his two-year-old sister, Nina, looking at his stretchies and booties, his pacifiers and rattles, his diapers, wondering how much longer they'd be at the doctor's and whether I should pack him a bag for the hospital that night, thinking that a baby with cancer made as much sense as an AK-47 making love, when the thought came to me that if I had any sense at all, I'd find a way not to love this kid.

I'd already had enough experience at living in the shadow of tomorrow's glare. I'd been fighting illness myself for seven years then—not an illness that threatened my survival, but one that had attacked my central nervous system and depleted my immunity, weakening my muscles and bathing my joints in pain. One that had ended my career as a lawyer, a just-beginning relationship, and my chance at having children—taking an eraser to the blackboard on which my future had been chalked. While it was possible that my health might improve someday, improvement wasn't promised to me, which left me stalked by the question of what future would replace the one I'd been sketching on that blackboard since childhood.

In the years that I'd been living with that question, I'd begun to envision myself standing at an elevator door, waiting for that future to arrive, fearing that when the door slid open, there'd be an empty shaft on the other side. I'd spent many days and even more nights haunted by the image of that vacuum. What I didn't need now, I told myself, rocking back and forth in Ethan's nursery, was more uncertainty and more fear—and so I decided what I'd do: "The baby," I would say, or "him," but never "Ethan." And whenever I was with him, I wouldn't fully be. I would blur my vision, my heart, my thoughts, my senses, to keep myself away. No more of this looking and listening, this holding and touching, this *noticing*—the curve of his cheek, the silk of his skin, the kiss of his head against mine. No.

Yes. Even now, I can see the first moment when Ethan said "yes." It was a few weeks after his diagnosis, and we were sitting on an orange vinyl couch—my sister, her husband, and I—waiting while he underwent a bone marrow aspirate before we checked him in for his next round of chemo. A nurse came over to us with more forms to be filled out, and just after the three of them had disappeared into an office, I looked up and there was Ethan, at the far end of the hall, draped over the arm of another nurse, with his stretchie un-snapped and his legs hanging out, hanging naked in the air, their softness silhouetted against the steel gray of the lab coat she wore. I looked at his face, at his scarlet nose, and knew he'd been crying hard, though he wasn't anymore.

As I moved down the hallway toward him, I could hear that he was now wailing instead, a distracted wail that un-derscored his searching, his looking back and forth, scan-ning the hallway—his looking past the doctors and nurses, the parents and children, the trays of equipment, the gur-neys, the X-ray machines—for any familiar thing to rest his eyes on. And then he saw me, and, for that instant, his face was filled with light. He reached out his arms and I gathered him into mine. And then he was screeching and I was say-ing, "Oh sweet baby, I know, I know. Tell me all about it. Tell me all *about* what they did to you in there," and he was clinging to my shirt and I was swaying back and forth and he was screeching on and on and I was "I know, I know"ing and he was reaching up to touch my face and I was kissing each of his fingers and then he was letting my voice and my swaying soothe his cries until slowly, slowly, slowly, they dwindled into whimpers. Yes.

After that there was a parade of others, those moments that left me no vote—that elbowed their way into view, stomped and whistled for my attention, tugged at my shirt and then at my heart, never offering me the option of turn-ing away: It is a month or so later, and I'm standing near his crib in Room 488, a few steps behind my sister, who's hold-ing his hands to the mattress while the nurse cleans the "central line" implanted in his chest. He is shrieking, razor-edged screams, struggling to pull his arms free, and so I step forward and lean over him, letting my hair brush across his forehead. At once silence permeates the room, with waves of relief flooding into the spaces where his shrieks had been rising and falling. He looks up at me, flutters his nowlashless lids, waits for me to do it again, and when I do, he laughs—the memory passing between us of those final weeks of Before, when it had become our ritual, every time I saw him, for me to lean, for him to flutter, for us to laugh. And so here, now, in this hospital room, with the masked face of a nurse hanging over him where his Winnie the Pooh mobile used to be, with electronic beeps and inter-commed voices replacing the lullabies he'd listened to then, with his scalp stripped clean of the hair he used to reach up and touch in response, I lean and he flutters and we laugh, the ritual swelling toward tradition, settling over us like a comforter of quilted flannel.

It is a couple of chemo rounds later, and my parents and I are keeping Ethan amused while my sister and her husband are in conference with his doctors. When he tires of crawl-ing up and down the length of his crib, and then of playing with his grandfather's eyebrows, with his grandmother's glasses, with a plastic Simba I've fished from one of his bags, we decide it's time for a walk. I strap him into his car seat, snap that onto a wheeled cart, and roll his IV pole over to push beside it—as automatic by now as if I were sliding him into a stroller, slipping on his jacket, making sure we'd re-membered to bring his juice cup along. As we start down the hall, I am thinking of how, the first time we stepped off the elevator onto this floor, it had been like stepping out of sum-mer sunshine into an unlit room; of how I had been able to see only the darkness that day, had been sure I'd never be able to distinguish anything else; of how, with time, I'd been able to identify shadows and shapes, objects and obstacles, and how now, these many weeks later, the details have grown clear—so that today, as we make our way down the hall, I no longer see frail, bald children with IV poles. Today what I see is Megan, headed for the playroom, followed by Eric and Natalie and John.

I look down at Ethan, who is looking around at the Four West wing—his playground and park; who is kicking his legs and waving his arms as we pass a gurney, the nurses' station, an oxygen tank, as though they were a slide, a playhouse, a tree; who squeals at children riding past in wheelchairs as though they were whizzing by on Schwinns—who has grown accustomed to the darkness before he ever had a chance to know the light. I stop the cart and stoop beside him, and he wraps a fist around my finger. I weave my other hand through the jumble of wires to smooth out his stretchie and straighten his bib, to wipe banana from his chin. "This isn't all there is," I whisper to him. "There's more, there's so much more," and he listens to me, looks at me, the one eye forced slightly forward by the tumor still shrinking behind it. He listens to me and looks at me. He hears and watches and believes me.

It is a Saturday afternoon a few months later, and Ethan is home, in a two-week hiatus between rounds of chemo. My sister decides to use the quiet of Nina's naptime to tend to the task of injecting "growth colony stimulating factor" into his central line, and while she's off gathering the equipment she'll need—the alcohol and the cotton balls, the infusion pump and the click lock, the white-blood-cell stimulator, premeasured in its syringe—I stand next to the changing table where he's lying. ("Make sure he doesn't roll off," she'd called over her shoulder as she was leaving the room, and "Of course," I'd answered back, hurrying over to stand by his side, both of us all the time knowing that he hasn't the strength to roll off, both of us all the time pretending that he does.) In the months since his diagnosis, he's absorbed bag upon bagful of chemo into his body, a drip at a time. I lean over him and smile, and he looks up at me, with his arms at his sides, with his legs lying limp.

"How's my Eth-man today?" I coo, and a smile flickers across his face. The wrinkled forehead. The scrawny neck. The translucent skin. I let my hair brush across the space where his eyebrows used to be, and the smile flickers past again, along with the eyelid flutter. I notice that he lets the part of the flutter when his lids are closed last a beat longer, resting, but I push on. "Hey Eth," I croon, "where's my nose? I bet you can't show me where my *nose* is!" and he reaches up one languid arm to touch it. Nothing more than the graze of moth wings against my skin, but there is this: a speck of light in his eyes, a longer-lasting toothless grin, a wiggle of one foot and then the other—each an embryo of a kick—and then, a hoarse whisper of laughter. Him, fighting back, insisting on going about the business of being a baby.

It is the day of Ethan's surgery, of the removal of the shrunken tumor from his adrenal gland, and we are all in the prep room, gathered around the last in a row of cribs, waiting. Ethan is being passed back and forth between his parents and grandparents, but when the anesthesiologist comes in, they group around her, and it is my turn. I carry him over to the window and stand there looking out, his head against my cheek, his arm around my neck. Dinosaurs, I promise him, and baseball. Halloween and mud puddles, butterflies and snowmen, the Good Humor man on muggy summer nights. Turning to look at him, I notice a vein, silver-blue beneath the skin of his scalp, and when I turn back to the window, I turn back knowing that the border separating universes is less than a centimeter wide, that it might be traveled in a splinter of a second.

On the street below, a car bleats its horn, and somewhere in the distance, a train whistle moans, and I think of all the life going on out there, beyond the farthest point we can see. I tell him that there are passengers riding that train and people waiting all along its route to meet it; that there are executives working in those skyscrapers there, and that beyond them, outside the city, truckers are heading cross-country, swallowing highway beneath their wheels; that there are people out there building houses and painting pictures, running races and conducting orchestras, plowing fields. I tell him that, at this moment, there are boatmen steering paddle wheels along the Mississippi and ranchers roping cattle across Montana's plains; that there are children chasing pigeons through St. Mark's Square. He pats my neck and I stroke his hand and we stay there for a time, looking out the window at the world he's only just come to.

When Ethan recovered from that surgery, he was declared "disease free," and it was then, as his months of treatment finally drew to an end, that I began to see that the moments I'd wanted to hide from as I rocked in his nursery that first day—the moments of daring to love him—had, in fact, become my refuge. At some point I had begun to wrap those moments around me, to wear them like cloaks, knowing that for as long as they lasted, they would shield me from whatever lay beyond—until, in time, whatever did lie beyond had begun to fade from view. In the months that followed, as our lives shifted back to the world outside the hospital's walls, as we moved from the agony of combat to the ache of watching, waiting, what if?ing, I continued to seek shelter from that fear and uncertainty within the borders of each of the moments I spent with Ethan. Looking back now, I see them like pearls, those moments, collected and stored in a keepsake box, each lustrous and whole and iridescent:

It is weeks after Ethan has returned home from surgery, from his final hospital stay, and my sister has dropped him at my house while she takes Nina to play with a friend. He has just begun to master the art of walking, and soon after he arrives, we open the front door and start down the path, with him just in front of me, a hand in each of mine, moving right foot, left foot, right foot out into the world; with me looking down at the top of his head, now covered with a layer of peach fuzz, and him pausing every few steps to grin up at me, his face luminous with awe at his achievement. The fourth time he does this, I surprise him by swooping down to kiss his cheek, and he laughs so hard, one hand slips from mine and he topples over, which makes him laugh harder.

Then he's back on his feet and we're on the road again—right foot, left foot, right foot—with me singing "Six Little Ducks That I Once Knew" and him squealing his approval, until we make it to our destination, a strip of fragrant lawn. Once we're seated side by side in the middle of it, though, with the grass prickly against his legs, his face grows serious, and he looks at me, then down at the ground, then up at me again, waiting for an explanation.

"That's grass, Eth," I say, pulling a blade and skimming it across his arm. "See? It won't hurt you. No way. It's not like those yucky needles. And now that we're all done with that nasty chemo and we don't have to worry so much about germs, you can touch it and walk barefoot in it any old time you want to. See?" I place the blade in his open palm, and he bends forward for a closer look. "Grass," I repeat, and he looks up and grins, then bends to inspect it again. Two squirrels run by, one chasing the other, and a chipmunk follows with a leaf in its mouth. A blue jay hops across the lawn and pauses, then ascends to sudden flight. The sun slips behind a cloud, softening the colors around us. And we sit there, side by side, inspecting a blade of grass—examining it, smelling it, turning it over—discovering the world within it, enveloped by a summer stillness that is knit of lawn mowers and cicadas, of birdsong and children's voices, of the rustle of leaves, of breeze.

It's a snowy afternoon several months later, and I'm sitting at the edge of the party room in my sister's building, watching fifteen four-year-olds try their hand at Bozo's Buckets. It's Nina's birthday party, and all the children are inches taller than Ethan, but he takes his place in line anyway, refusing to stand closer than the other children did, throwing the ball straight forward, sending it flying across the room, applauding himself, asking, "Where it goed?" applauding himself some more. But then: "Time to line up for Pin the Tail on the Donkey!" my sister announces, and as the children race past Ethan, one of them pushes him aside, sending him sprawling. He rights himself again and, turning toward me, starts to run, calling out, "Wawa!"—calling out his name for me.

He believes I can protect him, I think—from the pushes and the shoves, from the bullies and the bruises, from the monsters—and I realize that I want him to believe it, that *I* want to believe it, that for that instant, as he is running toward me, I do. But then that instant passes, and I know that all I can do is offer him all I have—the safety of this moment—a place on my lap with my arms around him, with soothing words murmured in his ear and a bag of Teddy Grahams in his hand; a place to gather himself before heading back into the party so that he'll be there, amidst the children and the blowers and the streamers and balloons, despite the pokes and the pinches, the stray elbows and knees, when the piñata bursts open and the goodies pour out.

It is summer again, and Nina and Ethan and I are coloring at their kitchen table while a thunderstorm hurls itself, in gusts, against the windows. Nina shows me the self-portrait she's working on, and Ethan pulls at my arm, wanting equal time. "Look, Wawa," he says, picking up a crayon and narrating as he draws. "I make de eyce. I make de noce." Nina and I applaud his every mark, but after his second picture is completed, he grows bored, climbs down from his chair, and wanders away. A moment later he is back, wielding a begonia. "Eth!" I say. "Where'd you get that?" And he points to a flowering plant across the room on the edge of my sister's desk, which is now sporting a prominent bald patch in its center. "Oh, Eth-man, you know better than that!" He grins and runs back to the desk, grabs hold of another bloom, and waves it back and forth, waiting. "He has his looking-for-trouble face on," Nina says, and goes back to her coloring.

I'm across the room before the flower is beheaded, wrestling it from his fingers, stroking the plant, stroking Ethan, saying, "We pat pat Mama's flowers. We NEVER hurt them." He watches and listens, his eyes wide, nodding, but when I step away from the desk, he grabs a fistful again. "Do you want me to take the flowers away?" I ask, and he shakes his head. "Then we pat pat," I say, showing him once more. He grins and grabs a bloom, and I wrestle it away, moving the flowerpot to a shelf high above him. "I wannit, I wannit, I wannit," he shrieks, his arms reaching for the heavens, his face a mask of tragic yearning. "Will you pat pat?" "Yes." The plant comes down. The fist goes out. The plant goes up. The shrieking starts. One more time: Down. Out. Up. Shriek. I go back to the table. "Sorry, Eth," I say, "but you have to learn that we just don't do that to Mama's plants." At once he is Hurricane Ethan, a snarl of limbs and wails and energy rolling across the kitchen floor, and I am a weather-caster, with nothing to do but watch and wait. But even as I cringe at his velocity and flinch at his volume, I am seeing us from a distance—I am seeing the miracle of us—any two-year-old, any aunt, any tantrum on any kitchen floor.

And then there comes *this* moment, in the park a few months later: Ethan is sailing toward me in the baby swing, all kicking legs and ruddy cheeks and windblown hair, and my arms are outstretched toward him, ready to send him sailing back again. I turn to look at the mothers around me—pouring juice into Barney cups and doling out boxes of animal crackers, untangling fights and retrieving balls, waiting at the bottoms of slides—and just as I am beginning to envision the elevator shaft again, to see the vacuum where my future had once been, Ethan calls out: "Lookit me. I'm a bird. Wawa, lookit me!" and I do. And when I do, the shaft and its darkness vanish.

I am back in the moment, suddenly knowing this: In daring to love Ethan, I've found a way to live with the shadow my own illness has cast across my life—to live, fully live, despite fear, despite uncertainty, despite the relentless throb of "what if?" In daring to love Ethan, I've learned to savor a Mozart sonata without listening for whether silence will follow, to cling to the grace of an October morning without giving December a thought, to drink in the golden light of a sunset without glancing ahead to see if I'm in for a starless night. In daring to love Ethan, I have learned to live now.

Yesterday Ethan asked me whether birds have birthdays too, and whether the sparrow that had just flown past us would also turn three next week. Before I could answer him, though, he was stooping to peer into the face of a poodle tied to a lamppost. "Hi, big dog," he said, and we moved on down the sidewalk. "Pat, pat," he announced a few moments later, reaching out to finger a row of tulips. "I pat patted the flowers," he reported to me. "I saw that," I said. "I'm proud of you for being so gentle," and this was his answer: "RED!" We'd reached the traffic light at the corner, and he'd stopped, leaning back as far as he could without toppling over, to cheer the arrival of each new color. The sixth time it turned green, I gave his hand a soft tug. "I think maybe we'd better get going," I said, and we made our slow way across the street, with me facing forward and him facing back, still watching the colors change. When we reached the other side, though, he turned around, just in time to see a butterfly flit past. "BU'ERFLY!" he shrieked, his feet leaving earth, and then stopped where he landed, in the middle of the sidewalk, to chant: "Bu'erfly, bu'erfly, fly away! You were a ca'erpillar yesterday!" I clapped and he grinned and we moved on. "Wawa, bu'erflies have birfdays too?" he asked, stopping again to wait for the answer. So that by the time we reached the bookstore, story hour was about to begin.

"Has everyone found a seat?" the teacher was asking as we stepped through the door, and Ethan dropped my hand to run across the room, where he forged a path through the legs of seated children until he reached the front row, found a spot on the carpet, settled himself, and looked up, ready to go. Half an hour later, the teacher turned the last page of

Chicka Chicka Boom Boom and set it down. "How about a round of the hokey pokey?" she asked, and Ethan leapt to his feet. He caught my eye through the crowd of rising children, grinned at me, and leapt again, landing square on his new white sneakers with the Velcro straps. "Boing," he said, and then grew solemn, waiting. "Everyone ready? Here we go," sang the teacher. "You put your right hand in. You put your right hand out. . . ."

From my chair across the room, I watched as Ethan thrust each hand and then each foot forward and back, then forward again, his eyes glued to the teacher's movements, his tongue peeking from the corner of his mouth, his face radiant with the union of joy and pride. Through a sudden blur of tears, I watched him—my wide-eyed, thigh-high, diaper-clad professor of survival—as he danced his way through the song, turning and jumping and shaking, then turning again, making his way through verse after verse to the grand finale:

> *You put your whole self in.*
> *You put your whole self out.*
> *You put your whole self in and you shake it all about.*
> *You do the hokey pokey and you turn yourself around.*
> *That's what it's all about.*

And as soon as that last verse had ended, as soon as he'd shaken himself about and turned himself around for the last time, he looked over to make sure that I'd been watching. *"Wawa!"* he called, weaving his way through the crowd, then running to throw his arms around my knees. *"Did you see me, Wawa? I putted your whole self in."* He leaned his head back, openmouthed with wonder, and I gathered him onto my lap, holding him close—holding the scent of his heat, the rhythm of his breaths, the beat of his heart next to mine. *"You sure did, sweet baby,"* I said. *"You sure did."*

SOME BIT OF LOVE TO CHEW ON

JOAN HALPERIN

My mother is the prima donna of the seventh floor, Doctors Hospital. Her flesh sags as her body shrinks at an alarming rate. She no longer bothers to put on the hand-sewn wig bought to cover her thinning hair. Maurice, her fourth husband, threatens not to visit if she "lets herself go."

She swears at the pain that sears her body. Sometimes she cries into the mirror. But she's expert at holding on to life. She won't let her heart stop beating.

Doctors from other floors flock to view her because she defies prognosis. She should be dead. She's the first on the agenda at the review meetings to determine if a patient should be sent home, stay at the hospital, or be sent to a nursing home.

My mother exceeds the time allotted to die. Out of compassion the committee votes to extend her stay.

"Why put the family through the turmoil of moving her now?" her doctors say at each meeting.

Two more weeks, the review board warns. Their patience is nearly exhausted. But she tricks them. Her heart catapults over hurdles, one beat after the other.

After work, I drive down from the Fair Haven Guidance Center where I teach psychotic children in a therapeutic nursery school. I race along the East River Drive, driven by a passion bordering on hate. Will she finally desert me without leaving a morsel, some bit of love I can chew on? I visit

every day. Usually I circle around and around, trying to find
a free parking space near the hospital. My mother wouldn't
do this if I were the sick one. She'd enter the most expensive
garage. She'd pay top dollar.

I can hear her boasting to an indifferent garage atten-
dant, "I don't know what time I'll be back. My daughter is
mortally ill." Tears, a dropped glove. Instant empathy from
a working-class man. My mother's style.

"Hello, Mom," I say as I tiptoe into her room.

"Don't use that hushed tone. Speak up," she orders.

I want to strike her down for not appreciating me. I want
to quiz her at a moment when her mind is registering clearly,
when she isn't under the haze of medication.

"What's my profession?" I want to demand. All these
years and she never remembers that I work with psychotic
children, that I'm a therapeutic teacher. She tells friends
that I work with the mentally retarded.

"Where exactly do I teach, Mom?" I want to ask.

"Isn't it wonderful? The patience Joan has to work with
the retarded. Such a sweet girl."

But I know she values the smarts, not the sweets. She believes my husband is one of the brightest men around. He's
a partner in a top-name law firm. Every few days she calls
him and demands that he rush right down to the hospital.

"You've got to come this minute," she says. "Bring those
power of attorney papers. I'll shift them from Maurice to
you. I want to protect Joan. Maurice will grab all the
money."

None of us knows that as she speaks, Maurice is
marching up and down Madison Avenue in a spending
frenzy. Diners Club and American Express cards zoom back
and forth between his palms and assorted cashiers on a nonstop journey. He is buying silk suits, handmade shoes, crates
of caviar. He sends a Tiffany watch to a niece in France. He
isn't about to let me inherit a dime.

Their anniversary is coming up in one month. After

eight years, he still retains his French accent. And he's charming in public: a fine raconteur, a smooth dancer. But soon after they married, he let my mother know he couldn't tolerate her friends: Etta, Lorraine, Rita, the members of her bridge club. Often he stormed into the apartment and broke up their games. He complained about money spent on the French espresso and delicate chocolate wafers she bought at Greenberg's bakery.

My mother is a manipulator, not a fighter. Frequently during those first months of marriage, she couldn't sleep nights. So she went to a sleep specialist who tried hypnosis. His office was on Fifth Avenue. Soothing relaxation tapes played in the waiting room.

One afternoon she and I met at the Plaza for lunch. A palm tree shaded our table. In a corner, a pianist played "Singin' in the Rain." The waiter stood at my mother's side. She ordered our usual: two bourbon sours and two Caesar salads.

"Is Maurice calming down?" I asked. "Are you getting enough sleep?"

"It's nothing," she said. "I'm not going to pay two hundred dollars for hypnosis when I can swallow a few Seconals. Two hundred dollars can buy us a dress at Bergdorf's."

"Buy who a dress?" I thought.

Since her hospitalization with uterine cancer, my mother has two doctors in daily attendance. In her mind, the good one is Dr. Silver and the bad one is Dr. Rogers. An expert at choosing the wrong man, she's mixed up who's good and who's bad.

Dr. Silver, the one she worships, prescribes all the pain medication she demands. He sits at the edge of the bed, pats her knees, and calls her a beauty. He suggests she wear her wig again.

"You're looking better today. Keep yourself gorgeous," he advises.

Thin and dark haired, he fluffs up a pillow, pulls the

shade. He records his visits in a date book before he leaves the room.

Dr. Rogers is more conservative. "We have to save the stronger doses of pain medication for the end," he advises me. "And why pressure her to wear a wig, for God's sake? Just keep her comfortable."

"Dr. Rogers is so unfriendly," she complains. "Such a cold human being. I love you, darling," she tells me. This is her style, intertwining hate with love. Playing us all against one another.

I sit on the bed and we hold hands. I lean against her chest. She is composed of butterfly bones. If I press too hard, she'll crumble. Stay. I don't want her to leave this world. She puts her arms around me, and for a second they feel substantial. They are solid and smell like wheat. Then poof! They become powder. Blown away by a sudden wind. She lets them rest at her sides.

"You'll be all right when I die," she says.

"You're not going to die," I respond.

"Don't be foolish. I want you to have my mink coat. Have it altered at Levy's this week. Otherwise," she starts to laugh, "I know you'll never wear it. Never even get to the tailor. Where's Maurice?"

"He's got a bad cold. He phoned just an hour ago. He'll be here as soon as it clears up."

"He detests illness," she says. "All those psychotherapists you went to, why on earth did you need them? I was the one with the real problems. Not you. Why on earth wasn't I enough for you?"

"You were too much," I almost say, but the new four-to-midnight nurse enters the room. We hire private-duty nurses around the clock. My mother wears them out. One moment they are trusted companions; the next day they are treated like incompetent maids. I know how they feel.

"Honey," the new private nurse speaks to my mother, "it's time for our nutrient."

"I am not a child, Sue Ellen. Sue Ellen, I want you to meet my daughter. She works with the mentally retarded."

"Hi," the nurse says. She is a willowy southerner who takes correction without getting ruffled. Her blond hair hangs long and crisp. "You all live around here?" she asks me.

"Mother in the city. Me in the country," I say.

"Well, hon, I gotta check your momma's temp and vitals. Give her an injection. So if you could just sashay down the hall and wait a little bit."

"She can stay," my mother commands.

I sit in the large green armchair in the corner. I've bought myself a pack of Pall Malls after fifteen years of not smoking. It's unopened in the bottom of my pocketbook. There's an ad that declares Pall Malls are cigarettes for real people. A tall, auburn-haired woman sits astride a horse while she puffs one. What I really want is to rush out to the corner coffee shop and light up. I want to inhale. I crave a chocolate fudge sundae. God, I want a smoke, a sundae, a bourbon sour. But I sit on the green chair like an obedient child and listen to my mother's urine tinkle into a bedpan. Then there's a sound of cavernous breathing—a wolf in her chest. And the final indignity of a hollow fart.

"You still going for counseling?" she calls out from a curtain that winds around the bed.

"Yup."

"Who's your doctor, may I ask?"

"No one you'd know."

"I asked a question. That's an evasion. Sue Ellen, are you fresh like that to your mother?"

"Honey"—I see Sue Ellen's silhouette behind the white curtain; it's as if she and my mother are starring in a shadow play—"honey, don't get upset or we just gonna ask your daughter to leave the room."

Sue Ellen's accent becomes sharper, carries more authority than it did when she entered.

"I simply asked my own daughter a question," my mother says.

"I'm gonna ask her to leave this room if you keep agitatin' yourself," Sue Ellen responds.

"Good," I think. "Order me out."

I want to whack my mother, throttle her. She knows how to dish out humiliation. If she had hair, I'd yank it out. A column of grievances long as a grocery list lines up in my mind.

Remember the time you forgot to pick me up at kindergarten. The time you lost my report card. The night you flirted with my date. Worse, the morning you said I was unfeeling, a statue.

"Remember your subway job?" my mother interrupts my thoughts. "I remember that day in your freshman year at Walden High when you were determined to become independent. You took a tin can with a Jewish orphan's picture on it and went down to the Eighty-sixth Street Lexington Avenue subway line to collect funds. Panhandling was what it was. Then you informed me you were working for a respectable charity." My mother's voice trembles.

And I recall running down those concrete subway steps, sure that I was starting a lucrative career. Oh, to liberate myself from her!

We start to laugh. She has managed to subvert Sue Ellen's authority.

"You made one quarter. And got chased out of three subway cars. One of those subway derelicts tried to grab your can away." My mother laughs and shakes in a palsied rhapsody behind the curtain. I laugh too, rock back and forth, clutch my belly.

Finally Sue Ellen yanks the curtain back. My mother lies in bed, freshly washed, smelling of Nivea lotion. She is powder fresh. Sue Ellen has combed down the sparse gray tufts of hair.

"I'm going to fetch your nutrient now," Sue Ellen says.

When she leaves, my mother beckons me over. "Don't forget the power of attorney forms. You've got to bring them down here."

She forgets how often she changes her mind about transferring authority. How afraid she is of Maurice. But she does trust me, after all.

Sue Ellen walks in the door balancing the chocolate nutrient on a tray.

"I'm not hungry." Mother's voice goes mushy.

"Just a few sips," Sue Ellen cajoles.

"A little." She sips through a straw that bends in half. "Bring something for my daughter," she says. "I bet she didn't have lunch."

"I'll get her a bacon, lettuce, and tomato sandwich," Sue Ellen says.

"Why, that would be grand! You know she works so hard. She was a case history herself. Me and all my husbands. And here she is teaching emotionally sick nursery school children. She's the only one in our family with a special degree."

"Special ed degree," I say.

"That's real good," Sue Ellen says. "Now don't tire yourself out," she tells my mother.

"It's probably some failure on my part that she gravitates to the mentally sick, don't you think? I never understood it."

I begin to cry. Tears run down my cheeks, my nose, into my mouth. I bend over, sobbing words I don't even understand.

"You knew all along what I do," I finally say.

"Darling." My mother's scalp shines luminous in the waning afternoon light. Her eyes are so dark, I want to cave into them and rest. "Don't give in," she says. "Stay strong and be smart. Now, call Levy's and get my coat altered."

JUKEBOX LAZARUS

RHONDA C. POYNTER

This is a simple one—just a few observations about when Jr. died—really died, honest to God above. Nobody *believes* that he died; after all, he's died so many times before that just about anybody who knows Jr. figures he's hiding out in Chicago or St. Louis or somewhere, and hell, I'll tell you right now that I didn't see a body. But Mom said that she's working on getting me a copy of the death certificate, and maybe then that will put all doubts to rest.

Personally, I think that he's really gone this time. No, I don't believe that Elvis is running a truck stop this side of Kansas City, but I do believe in energy and auras and all that kind of thing, and Jr.'s energy just isn't around anymore. I can feel it in my bones, the way he'd feel it in his bones which pony to play on a Saturday night, or which red line to pick out on the map when we were down to our last five dollars and a half tank of gas, and the baby was crying for more than milk from our sickly, anemic mother.

Jr.—I'll call him Dad in private conversation, but I tend to call him Jr. at all other times, although I'm not quite sure why (a shrink told me once that I subconsciously needed the world to know that I lived with, Jesus, I *survived* Jr. Poynter!)—anyway, Jr. first began dying, to my recollection, it was the 1960s. We kids were all around six or so except for Mona, the baby; that sticks in my head because people always felt so bad for a woman with a new baby whose husband had just managed to go out and get himself killed. I'll bet that Jr. just about had a heart attack when Mona started growing and Mom couldn't have any more kids.

We were always living in some little watering hole like Pekin, Illinois, or Owensboro, Kentucky. This was another thing that I didn't really understand about Jr.: It seemed to me, even as a ten-year-old kid, that if you were going to blow into town long enough to set up camp, charge everything all over town, run up bills and never pay the rent, and then blow back down the road about four months later, you'd choose a big city or somewhere that didn't make your home address and face so accessible. Not Jr.—he'd plunk us down across the street from the goddamned landlord, and it took roughly six weeks before we kids were having to go to school and hear, "Your daddy don't pay my daddy the rent, and my daddy says you ain't nothing but white Georgia trash!"

But Jr. never did do what others might see as common-sense actions. I can't help but wonder just what in the hell he might be doing to the great beyond right about now. Can angels have breakdowns?

That's how I remember my entire childhood going. We'd come home from whatever school we had been dumped into for (if we were lucky) a quarter of the year, toss our books on the kitchen table, and yell up the stairs to Mom's bedroom, "Hey, the principal sent us home early. He says there's an emergency. Did Dad die again?" Most times he had, and we were down the road again.

We would meet up with Jr.—obviously risen again like some jukebox Lazarus, put your quarter in and tell him where the next little town was—waiting at this or that truck stop, leaning up against a telephone booth at a Greyhound station, sitting way down low in the front seat of the car he'd run over the state line in hopes that the finance company wouldn't be able to find him and repossess it.

I saw my father cry about two things in his lifetime—losing his Thunderbird to the finance guy, and when my brother Ronnie died. And I remember thinking, neither one of these things had to happen. He could have paid for the car with a fraction of the money he wasted on racetracks and get-rich schemes and eating out every night, and my brother—well, he could have let us get Ronnie some help. I had a hard time feeling sorry for Jr. for the longest time, bitter as I was about Ronnie's suicide, thinking that it was mostly to get the hell out of that family and the way we had to live, but now I understand something about Jr. He just didn't know how to do the right thing. He wouldn't have been able to make the right choice to save his own soul, no matter how badly he wanted to, and when I finally comprehended this fact about my father's character, I quit hating him.

"See, Ronnie, there's Dad. He's not dead," I'd say to my brother as Mom swung the battered station wagon into whatever parking lot to claim our father; Ronnie would wipe his eyes and blink, and Christ, that's what I remember about my baby brother. Always confused and lost.

"He's just pretending he's dead so the bill collectors don't come looking, or the cops. Come on, he'll live forever, Ronnie, for chrissakes." And as far as my brother knew, I was right about that. He beat Jr. to the grave by almost ten years.

I've always personally believed that Jr. truly died the day my brother died. I don't know what in the hell kept him alive for another decade, because it couldn't have been a simple beating heart. His had been so shattered—it sounds like one of those god-awful country songs he was always wailing as we barreled down the highway, but it's a fact—his heart had been so destroyed by Ronnie's death that there couldn't have been anything left to function. I began to think that maybe he had taken his Lazarus image a little too seriously.

So you've got to understand my attitude now, my sort of sitting-back-and-taking-stock-of-the-situation attitude. I do believe he's dead, but I just can't act like I guess I should be acting. Maybe I used up all my real feelings years ago when I had to cry on cue and tell the bill collectors, "My daddy's gone to heaven and my mama's real sick." I could sob right through the unfortunate bill collector scribbling PAID across the bill and shoving it at me, telling me to give it to my mama; if I could bring up the hiccups and trembling, I'd get a ten-dollar bill or more out of the performance for my-self. I'd be sitting down at the 7-Eleven with a fistful of candy bars and a movie magazine by the time the mark got home and told his wife he hated his job and that he was go-ing to go back to selling shoes; God, I was good. Jr. used to tell me that Hollywood didn't know what it was missing while I sat down on some one-horse farm in Fort Worth or in a trailer park out in Crown Point, Indiana.

Maybe it was because he was so sick for so long that I can't find it in myself to carry on and wring my hands. Since Ronnie died, Jr. had been trying to kill himself every single day, and he just kept on trying until one night the perfect mixture of whiskey and too many pills threw him into a coma that stuck his ass in a nursing home for the next ten years. And he still didn't die. Christ, talk about believing your own publicity.

But here he's finally gone, and it's been a month now, and I guess I'm coming to grips with it. I suppose, in hind-sight, that I should have gone home for the funeral, but I just couldn't do it, and I think that Jr. would have understood. I have buried him so many times before in my mind, my heart—I didn't need to do it again. I know he's gone, no matter who is already whispering, *Ah, hell, he's jumped bond and he's in Detroit. . . .*

I'll tell you something, and that will put the subject to rest. The night my mother called and told me, I bundled up my boy because these California nights get cold early-on this time of year, and we walked on out to the hill that over-looks the entry to the interstate. It took a bit because his legs are so small, but we got there and sat down, and we spent the next hour just watching the cars blow by, the lights rolling on and on into the distance. It got so dark that all we could see were the high beams and the hitchhikers they illuminated, but still we sat, and there was this one guy holding up a sign, his backpack dropped on the pavement beside him. I'll tell you what that sign said, even though we couldn't see it. It said ANYWHERE, and the guy probably looked just like my father did twenty, twenty-five years ago. He probably smoked Pall Malls and thought that Hank Williams was the finest poet to ever come down the pike. And we watched until a long hauler finally groaned to a stop and threw open the passenger-side door for the guy. He jumped in and they disappeared down the highway, and that, I swear to God, *that* was the very moment I knew that Jr. was really gone. Something got on that truck with that stranger and went, and it just kept going, even after the truck driver had pulled over in Santa Fe for some sleep. Something found that piece of road that we're not allowed to see yet, I know it.

And damn it, I'll tell my son, no matter what you hear as you're growing up, no matter what others will try to put into your head because they need to believe their stories, your grandfather really did die, just a few weeks ago, at the age of fifty-six. I can feel it in my bones this time—just the way he felt it in his bones which pony to play and which direction on the map to take. Just the way Jr. did.

THE RACE

MARIA EXPOSITO GLASS

Everybody seemed to be poor, like us, in the small French village where I grew up—except for those few families who lived behind the great stone walls with broken glass bottles cemented at the top. My parents' speaking Spanish in public did not embarrass me until junior high, and my dad wasn't yet scared of my growing up.

Every once in a while, the village would throw a party, no invitations required, usually to honor some unknown fallen soldier or the storming of a prison. The carnival would come to plant its tents in the marketplace with its symphonies of noises, its greasy smells and bulging lights. Games and competitions were organized with small monetary prizes for the fastest kids in town.

Growing up, I was eager to participate, but Mom had trouble letting go of my hand and would always decide I was too small to compete. Until one Fourteenth of July, when I was six or maybe seven, I escaped from her grip. I planted myself on the line in the middle of the big kids, the ones who pushed me around on the playground, the ones spreading the rumors that I had lice. Mom tried to remove me, but I firmly stood my ground. "I want to run too," I begged. She was holding my brother Paquito tugging on the other side, and I was too big already for only one hand. Then my father stepped in.

"*Déjala, mujer.* Today she can run."

"*Pero*, Paco. She's too small, and you're gonna have to

get her and carry her around." She tried to reach one more time, but Paquito was winning the round.

Dad kneeled, the man who would never put his knees on the ground. His blue eyes looked at me through the thick glasses. He didn't touch me. (Fathers don't touch.) "If you want to run, it's all right, but under one condition: I will not go and get you if your side hurts or if you fall. If you start running, you will finish this race." I nodded, not so sure anymore. What if I ran out of breath, or if my belly would ache? But I nodded, and I knew there was no turning back.

I set my fifty pounds of bones between two mountains of kids who covered the sky. *"A vos marques? Prêts? Partez!"* And we took off, fifty-odd mad kids competing for one prize. I started as fast as I could, afraid already I would not finish. The crowd lined up on the street walks. I knew I had to go all the way to the fabric factory, then make a U-turn at the curve and come back on the other side of the road to end where I had started.

Halfway before the turn I was running alone, trying to catch up with the rest of the troop. A few boys were already on their way back, smirking at me through teeth clenched by the effort. But I tried not to look, and I kept running in my Sunday shoes. I finally reached the U-turn where some already had quit. My tongue had doubled in size. I felt the first pang on my right side as the first runners reached the finish line. For a few seconds, I wondered if I could stop and just walk slowly with my belly in my hands. I tried to spot the face of my father in the crowd, maybe to ask for his permission to fail. But still I was too busy running toward the foggy line.

Then I heard the crowd cheering louder as this big girl came strolling back from the finish line. "You can quit now. It's over." She kept running slowly next to me, not even breathing hard. "You can quit now, Maria. They're gonna give you a prize just for being the last one." I didn't look at her. *I'll show you. I'll show you.* And I started running harder to get away from her. The cheers became louder as I approached the line. The crowd had not scattered yet, still waiting to see the last one arrive.

Finally, I could see Dad, this time towering on the skyline with his arms wide open, whispering something that only I could hear: *"Vamos, vamos."* He stepped out of the crowd and pushed back the finish line one gigantic step farther. *"Vamos, vamos."* Silent words only I could hear. I collapsed in his arms, my heart touching his heart. He didn't kiss me. (Fathers don't kiss.) But he raised me to the sky before I could stop panting. I rested my belly against his head, and he rubbed my pulsing pain with his baldness as if he knew where it hurt. Then, he carried me inside the bar to receive my prize, *a hombros*, like a bullfighter who had just completed the right *faena*. He set me in front of the table, said, "Here is my daughter," in his butchered French, and it sounded like praise.

The prize was small, but it was still a prize. They said I deserved it because the race was so long and I seemed so small. The money was quickly spent. I bought my brother some cotton candy and my mother a plastic ring from one of the machines. I don't remember the rides.

Since then I have started many races—some with the finish line already drawn for me, some I had to first set, and some I could not even see. But each time, when I run out of breath, when my belly aches and I look for his face, I remember my father: "You will finish this race."

THE NIGHT AHEAD

JOAN SHADDOX ISOM

Here by your own choice, not wanting to be a burden, as you say, your days are a routine worn into stained linoleum by shuffling feet, squeaking carts bearing cold food, medication and instructions: The white pill and eye drops at 7:00 A.M. Heart pill at noon, and the antacid if supper sits heavily on the stomach.

In between there is Horace from the church, but he does not know what to say to a ninety-six-year-old woman. Your children try. We ask what you would like to eat. When the winds warm in March, you inquire about the wild greens. I scour the fence rows, finding nothing but polk, and I'm afraid its acrid taste would upset your stomach. I buy spinach at the grocer, cook it, and carry it to you in an insulated bowl. You eat it without comment. I fear your taste buds went with your eyesight and your hearing, but your mind still catalogs where each child and grandchild lives, their birth dates, which schools they attend, and when they are expected for a visit.

"Do you know any news?" you greet me each time I visit. Despite your diminished hearing, your failing sight, you still know more about the family than any of your children. You extract bits and pieces from each of us and put them together in a litany to recite to the next one who stops by:

> Martha is in a family way
> Troy is on a fire detail

Carl is planting garden
Lynda has a new job in Dallas
And Dorothy might be washed away
By all the rain in California.

You ask if I like my daughter's new boyfriend, and I say yes, but I've been fooled before. You admonish me, telling me there are plenty of good people in the world. We could debate this, but your deafness and your refusal to wear a hearing aid leaves us with no abstractions, no long conversations of the soul. To let you speak without interruption is the best approach.

You inquire about your house, empty on the edge of town. I assure you we'll see to the water pipes in the subzero weather, but your voice is strangely detached. After you moved to the nursing home, I saw you begin to draw your life into the small circle that surrounds your bed, letting go of your house and its furnishings, keeping only some of your clothing, your jewelry and a few keepsakes. Your people are still important, but I can't help but think that you've cultivated a disinterested space as a protective veneer between yourself and the physical world as you slowly inch your way out of it.

You suspect your treasures are being stolen, so I rig a piece of your luggage to lock, thread a purple ribbon through the key for you to keep. You touch each piece before I close the lid. Your fingers have memorized their shapes: gifts from your grandchildren, cameos, dime-store pins (worn like proud little flags, a different one each day, at the throat of your cotton dresses), your wedding ring—a gold band now nesting in a curl of bright beads. You look in triumph at the nurse as you encircle your neck with the purple ribbon, dropping the key down the front of your dress.

I walk you up the hall and you hold to me reluctantly, unsteady on your feet but too proud, I suspect, to want help.

We pause before a doorway and look in. They are stripping the room, dumping the contents into plastic bags.

"That old man died this morning. They rolled him out while I was down at the desk waiting for my mail," you say. Your casual tone chills me, but you seem to be on easier terms with death than I. You've survived most of your friends. Your firstborn, a phantom brother to me, died as an infant years ago, although you seldom speak of him. For the last thirty-eight years, you've been a widow, living, my brother pointed out, longer without your husband than you lived with him. You grieved with me when my son, your grandson, died. "He came to see me, brought me a box of crackers the day before he died," you said, before you gave up trying to find words of comfort.

Back in your room, you tell me to turn over the new month on your calendar. It's been years since you could see the numerals; still you insist. Your clock sits close by on your dresser, and each night you ask me to wind it. You hold it inches from your face trying to see the hour. It seems important that you know when and where you are.

One evening in mid-August, I move through the stifling heat without feeling it. I have an impossible duty to perform. I must try to break the news that your eldest child, my sister, has lost her battle with cancer. Your courage shames me, immersed in my own grief. I try to embrace you, but part of you will not succumb. You hold yourself straight and rigid. I'm beginning to understand this behavior. It's the admonition that clenches your heart and jaw and fists as it clenches mine: "Don't fall under the weight of grief lest you can't get back up." It has braced my own backbone for good or ill since my own child's death. You told me once, "The only time I ever had to send word to your father to come home was when one of your brothers was just born and he got an infection in his belly button." You saw my father only every two months or so, back from his work in the forest. In between, you coped with five children and the day-to-day conflicts of a large family with a rigidity that held you—held us—together.

You birthed me long after you thought you'd had your last child. The rest of your children share a history with you that I don't: Pleasant Hill Ranger Station; Sand Gap; Pruitt, Arkansas; Deadwood, South Dakota—all places you lived while my father worked for the Forest Service. Sometimes you cooked outside. I have a photo of you on the banks of Little Rapid Creek. You are wearing overalls and holding a skillet over a campfire. If my math is correct, I would be born five months later. I don't remember the sparkler almost catching the tent on fire on the Fourth of July; I don't recall my sister being caught by a wolf trap. "You weren't born yet," you always say, when telling me some family story. History and time cut a chasm between us.

But now, before the supper carts creak through, the two of us sit on the edge of your bed and hold each other, conjoined by our terrible bond. Neither of us had planned to outlive any of our children. Neither of us knows what to do next. This time I'm the one struggling to find the right words. Softening your pose, you reach over and stroke my hair as if I were seven years old again. We are quiet for a moment, then you find the right and true words that somehow venerate us both. *"You know . . . only you know."*

I don't want to leave you. I know the unspeakable loneliness of the night ahead when the lights are turned out and you are left with the infinite void that the death of a child brings. When I finally say good night, you pull my head down to feel my face with your fingertips, but not too closely. I think you yearn to see me still smooth-skinned and big-eyed in youth. I think you need (for my sake) to distort time and distance between where I am and where you so want me to be.

OUSIA

THE REALNESS OF THINGS

MADELEINE L'ENGLE

I learned several years ago that a four-generation summer can be a good one only if we all have our own survival routines. Each one of us must manage to find a time of solitude and privacy. Hugh, when he is in Crosswicks, goes to his garden. Alan goes out to the Tower to read and write. I do not want to take my pain out on the rest of the family, so every afternoon, before time to cook dinner, I go across the fields to the brook, pushing through the tall grass nearly ready for its first haying, with the dogs circling joyfully about me. When I am out of sight Mother is apt to send for me. "Where's Madeleine? Get Madeleine." At the brook I'm beyond the reach of even a loud shout. If anybody really wants me, somebody has to come fetch me.

I used to feel guilty about spending morning hours working on a book; about fleeing to the brook in the afternoon. It took several summers of being totally frazzled by September to make me realize that this was a false guilt. I'm much more use to family and friends when I'm not physically and spiritually depleted than when I spend my energies as though they were unlimited. They are not. The time at the typewriter and the time at the brook refresh me and put me into a more workable perspective.

Across the brook is a stone bridge; it is not a natural bridge; it was put there a century or more ago by skillful hands and no modern stone-moving tools. It was probably part of one of the early roads, barely wide enough for a single horse and rider. I sit on it and dangle my legs over the gentle flowing of the water, shaded by maple and beech, birch and ash trees. I need perspective, and how to find it? caught in the middle of things, never quite able to avoid subjectivity, or to get the thinking me and the feeling me to coincide.

This makes me confused, makes me lose sight of reality. I feel my lacks as a wife, daughter, mother; and if I dwell too much on my lacks they become even greater, and I am further from—not just reality, but the truth of this summer. Will I ever know it?

When Josephine was just a year old, I spent most of the summer alone at Crosswicks because Hugh was off working at various summer theatres, and Mother had broken her ankle in the spring and so could not join us until August. During these solitary weeks I wrote a full first draft of a book. It was my fourth full-length novel, and I had reluctantly put the third on the shelf, after many revisions; so I felt especially precarious about the summer's work, and I knew that how I would feel about that particular summer for the rest of my life was going to depend on what happened with my manuscript.

The book was well received by the publisher and—eventually—the press, and is still, after all these years, selling. And so, I remember that summer as a "good" summer. If the book had been rejected, it would be forever in my memory as a "bad" summer. That's irrational, but it's the way things are.

So what of the verisimilitude of that long-gone summer? Do I know it at all? It was a time of solitude, rather than loneliness, because I was happy with my writing, happy with my baby. But what was it *really* like? I don't know.

So I will probably never fathom the reality of this summer. What is the truth of the ninety-year-old woman waiting for me at the house, who is changed beyond recognition and yet who is still my mother?

For a human being, truth is verisimilitude, a likeness to what is real, which is as close as we can get to reality. It has taken me many years to learn that reality is far more than meets the human eye, or ear, or mind, and that the greatest minds have never attained more than fragmentary flashes of what is really real.

Below me on a flat, mossy stone in the brook sits a small green frog. What is a frog? What is the reality of a frog? I was fascinated by a scientific article which showed pictures of a frog as seen by a human eye, by a bird's eye, by a snake's eye. Each saw a very different creature. Which frog was more real?

All of us in Crosswicks this summer see a different person when we look at my mother. Vicki and Janet and Margie have known her all their lives, as Jo's and Maria's and Bion's grandmother. For my children, she has been a very special grandmother. When Josephine had mononucleosis the first winter of her marriage, she didn't get well until she was sent down to Grandmother to be petted and pampered and cosseted. Bion, each spring vacation, says, "I have to go South for a week with Grandmother." I know a very different person from the one my children do. I know only a fragment of this old lady. She is far more than I can begin to understand. She was fifty-five when my father died; the woman he was married to for nearly thirty years is not the woman I know. I have pictures of her when she was a baby, a young girl, a bride, but this past of my mother's is beyond my comprehension. I am far from understanding her reality.

The Greeks come to my help again; they have a word for the realness of things, the essence of a frog, of the stone bridge I am sitting on, of my mother: *ousia*.

If I am to be constant in loving and honoring my mother I must not lose sight of *ousia*. It's a good word; it's my new word. Last summer my word was *ontology*: the word about being. This summer I need to go a step further, to *ousia*, the essence of being, to that which is really real.

The frog makes a small, clunking noise and hops to another stone and sits, his pale green throat pulsing. He *is*: frog: unworried by the self-consciousness with which the human animal is stuck; it is our blessing and our curse; not only do we know, we know that we know. And we are not often willing to face how little we know.

I learn slowly, and always the hard way. Trying to be what I am not, and cannot be, is not only arrogant, it is stupid. If I spend the entire day hovering around Mother, trying to be the perfect daughter, available every time she asks, "Where's Madeleine?"; if I get up early with my grandbabies and then stay up late with my actor husband and get no rest during the day; if I have no time in which to write; if I make myself a martyr to appease my false guilt, then I am falling into the age-old trap of pride. I fall into it too often.

A conversation with a friend helped open my eyes. Connie is about ten years older than I am, and her mother died a year ago, and Connie is filled with guilt. Now I happen to know that Connie was more than just a dutiful daughter; she kept her mother at home until a hospital was inevitable; she visited her daily thereafter; the difficult old woman was treated with love and kindness; and I told Connie that if anybody had little cause for guilt, it was she. But the guilt was obviously there, and a sore weight. So I said that we all, all of us without exception, have cause for guilt about our parents, and that I had far more cause than she. Then I heard myself saying, "I don't think real guilt is ever much of a problem for us. It's false guilt that causes the trouble." Connie gave me a funny, surprised look, and said, "I think you're right."

And a load of guilt fell from my own shoulders.

I certainly have legitimate cause for both real and false guilt with my mother. But when I try to be the perfect daughter, to be in control of the situation, I become impaled on false guilt and become overtired and irritable.

It is only by accepting real guilt that I am able to feel free of guilt as I sit on the stone bridge and cool my feet in the dappled shade and admire the pop eyes of the frog; and it comes to me that if I am not free to accept guilt when I do wrong, then I am not free at all. If all my mistakes are excused, if there's an alibi, a rationalization for every blunder, then I am not free at all. I have become subhuman.

At best I am far from a perfect wife, or mother, or daughter. I do all kinds of things which aren't right, which aren't sensitive or understanding. I neglect all kinds of things which I ought to do. But Connie made me realize that one reason I don't feel guilty is that I no longer feel I have to be perfect. I am not in charge of the universe, whereas a humanist has to be, and when something goes wrong, tiny, delicate Connie, like most convinced humanists I've known, becomes enclosed with self-blame because she can't cope with the situation, and this inability presents her with a picture of herself which is not the all-competent, in-control-of-everything person she wants to see.

It is a trap we all fall into on occasion, but it is particularly open to the intelligent atheist. There is no God, and if there is, he's not arranging things very well; therefore, I must be in charge. If I don't succeed, if I am not perfect, I carry the weight of the whole universe on my shoulders.

And so the false guilt which follows the refusal to admit any failure is inevitable.

STUDYING PERSPECTIVE ON A SATURDAY AFTERNOON

BARBARA BRENT BROWER

Chicago's Michigan Avenue seemed a zillion miles long to you, that twelve-year-old girl with skinny legs and thick brown braids, trudging from the Art Institute across the Chicago River, past the Wrigley Building, the Tribune Tower, past all the stores that became progressively more expensive as you got closer to your father's bookstore. You could have taken a bus, but you were afraid of missing your stop, so every Saturday after art class you would walk, your heavy portfolio, made of yellow oilcloth stretched over cardboard and fastened together with red Mystik tape, tucked under your left arm where the edges dug into your armpit, toward that vanishing point on your horizon.

You were learning about truth, beauty, and perspective as they were reflected in art. After class, you struggled down Michigan Avenue to have lunch with your father, who had divorced you and your mom and little brother four years earlier to begin a new life and a new family, for reasons that were never clear to you. You just understood it was very important to your father that you, your brother, and your mother had never existed. Never.

Oh, he admitted to you in private, during those sacred, secret Saturday lunches, that it was wrong, but what could he do? He wanted to succeed in a world and with a woman who had wealthy parents who did not approve of divorce. Your mother's family was also wealthy, and your grandfather did not approve of divorce either, but the real difference was that he did not approve of your father; thought he was a gold digger.

In order for your father to have these new in-laws support him in his dream of owning the finest bookstore in the world, you could not have ever been born. Dreams are so fragile, so special, how could you, he said, how could you with your little selfish, stupid needs spoil all that for him? So you obediently faded into the furthest corner of his life and became his silent secret. Your brother was only five when your father left, too young for memories. But you were his "Little Princess," his much-loved firstborn, so you had a unique bond you could not give up. You had to believe in him.

He kept saying that he had to gain some perspective on his situation. He kept promising that everything would work out in time, that someday you could be his daughter again; your brother, his son . . . someday, when he had enough success, enough money to ride above the scorn that was sure to come when what he had done to get to the top was revealed. But he wasn't ready yet, not where he wanted to be. He would be, though. Someday.

Each Saturday you wondered if he had gained that perspective yet and would be able to see the world from your twelve-year-old point of view. But each Saturday was the same, except the restaurants kept changing. Once it was Köngsholm with its puppet opera on the second floor. Once, Rick's, where the owner wore a black cape and kept a chest of money in his office for his friends to use when they were a little short. Once it was the Oak Room at the Drake Hotel. Wherever it was, whenever someone recognized him and came over to the table, he would introduce you as his niece, and you would smile your frozen-face smile, feeling the freeze burn all the way down to your toes.

Maybe today would be different. You knew what you had to do, but your heart kept hitting your chest wall, making it ache. You put your head down, readjusted the portfolio that contained your latest work, *Blue Horses in the Snow,* that had gotten the top grade, a *star,* on top of your other sketches. Maybe he'd be proud.

You observed others walking along those zillion miles of Michigan Avenue. You wondered if perspective was important to them, or beauty, or truth, but you couldn't tell. They shuffled along lost in thought, but they seemed to know where they wanted to be in their lives. They brushed by you, not realizing that you did not exist. You wanted them to stop and take a look around, to acknowledge you as being as solid as the buildings that rose against the sky like hands with long fingers. You wanted to cry out, "Here, here I am! I exist! I am taking up space just the way you do!"

You wanted them to see the beauty of the lake, sapphire that day, sparkling between the buildings on the right, across Lake Shore Drive. You wanted them to see the beauty of the river, lovely in the hazy afternoon even with flotsam bumping against the bridge abutments.

From your perspective, high on the bridge, the sun-sequined garbage added—what had they called it in class? Oh, yes, "visual interest." If your portfolio had not been so heavy and hard to manage, you would have opened it right there in the middle of the bridge, pulled out your sketch pad, found the pencil in your blue Indian Head cotton skirt pocket, and made a sketch in the manner of Monet. You were studying his water lily paintings that took up whole walls at the Art Institute. Studying the way the flowers were there, hiding in all that color, the perspective always shifting. You would have named your masterpiece *Garbage on the Chicago River Hidden by Light.*

You wanted to tell your father about what you had learned in class that day about Monet, about the vanishing line; about how, as you drew closer to someone, it was as if he got farther away. Maybe today you could change his perspective for the good of everyone.

You wished you could fathom the authors and philosophers he admired: Sartre, Proust, Mann. He had read you *The Little Prince,* but you guessed literature did not apply to real life, or else how could he love Saint-Exupéry and do what he continued to do? How could a father do such things, except that his dream was everything, and nothing else was, and you had the mission of helping him achieve his dream?

The Saturday conversation was always the same. He wasn't interested in your pet crayfish, Dopey. It always went: "Wellyoulookfinehow'syourmotherbrotherareyougetting goodgradescan'tfigurewhyachildofmineishavingproblems withmathit'sEASYFORMEYOUAREN'TSTUPID AREYOU?Wellstudyharderhurryupfinishyourlunch don'tslurpyoursodaIhavepeopleIMPORTANTPEOPLE comingintwentyminutesaren'tyoufinishedyetHERE'S SOMEMONEYGOBUYYOURSELFSOMETHING ONYOURWAYHOMEhaveyourmomcallthestorewhen yougethome . . . sheknowsthesignalgottagogood-byesee younextSaturdaydon'tCRYallthiswillworkoutsomeday you'llseenowbegoodandrunalong."

It was just a matter of perspective. You adjusted your skirt and blouse and rubbed your sweaty hands on your socks as you pulled them up, carefully positioning your portfolio under your sore arm one more time.

You pulled the shop door open and stepped inside. The place was so beautiful. The blue and red bindings, the glint of gold along page edges, all those glorious books filled with all those splendid words.

"Take heart," you told yourself as you placed your portfolio against the leg of a table just inside the front door. The table was loaded with books on art.

You took a deep breath and blurted out the forbidden phrase: "Hi, Dad, I'm here!"

His face became almost purple. "I told you never to call me that in public! There are people here. *Important* people who wouldn't understand, who could take money away from this business, force me to miss my support payments to your mother. Do you want that? Did she put you up to this? Wait till I call her. You've ruined everything. I can't today, can't today, can't . . . here's ten dollars. Just take it and go!"

Your face felt slap-scarlet, then I–am–dead gray. You refused to cry. You shut off your heart and took the bill out of his hand. You locked your throat down tight. You took that bill and tore it into a zillion bits of green and tossed them in his furious face. You stood, turning into one of those statues at the Art Institute, hearing all those marvelous books rustle their pages in anger as customers gaped.

Truth and beauty would have to wait. Someday would never come. That is the problem with perspective.

MAXINE KUMIN

Victor and I met through mutual friends on a blind date on the seventeenth of April, 1945. It was Patriots' Day weekend, a holiday previously unknown to me, but a significant one in Massachusetts. Schools and many businesses there close in honor of the midnight ride of Paul Revere; tradition has established that the annual Boston Marathon be run on that holiday.

In common with many of his classmates who had gone off to serve in World War II, Victor missed graduation. He had been granted a Harvard diploma at midsemester in 1943. Now he was a staff sergeant in the army, a rather unprepossessing rank in my eyes. All three of my brothers were officers. Home on a ten-day furlough from a place in New Mexico that I had never heard of—Los Alamos—he was extremely vague about what he did there, though he did tell me that he had been in infantry training in Alabama and somehow got transferred. I didn't know enough to ferret out the mystery.

A serious history and lit major, a dean's list Radcliffe junior, I was wearing, according to the custom of the time, my quasi-boyfriend's navy ensign's gold bar pinned to my sloppy-joe sweater. I had been going out with—"seeing," we called it then—my navy man for three years, ever since we met as counselors at adjoining summer camps in the Berkshires. He was blond and rather good looking. His manners were impeccable. A man of the world, he had slid through Harvard with gentleman's C's but felt that his future was assured. My mother doted on him. I was grateful when he shipped out on his destroyer to shepherd convoys crossing the Atlantic. The chemistry between us was wrong; I felt uneasily that I was being pressured to make a commitment to someone who was nothing more than a friendly date.

Victor and I saw each other for five days in a row. There was then and continues to be no explanation for our instant and mutual attraction. Looking at a snapshot taken that following summer, I see how darling we were, he lean and saturnine in a white T-shirt and baggy khakis snugged tight with a belt, I in a fashionable striped bathing suit and smoking a very sophisticated cigarette. My shoulder-length hair is wavy and dips over one eye in the style of a long-forgotten movie star. There's something raffish, sexually provocative and at the same time vulnerable, about the two kids in that photo. We look as though we belong together; in fact, we are flaunting it. But did we have any idea of the future we were letting ourselves in for?

During those five days in April 1945, I think Victor came to some of my classes, for even in my newly besotted state, I wasn't about to cut any lectures; once, I remember, he came to the dorm for dinner. Dinners back then were formal affairs. We had to wear skirts, we stood behind our chairs until the housemother entered and took her seat, and I think we even said a few words of grace, a practice I have come to resent, almost to detest. Why do agnostics and atheists have to pay lip service to belief?

Biddies, for that was how the mostly Irish maids were known, served each table. The biddies were our dear friends and confidantes; they cleaned our rooms and mooned over the framed pictures on our bureaus and mothered us in ways that college students today would find quaint if not politically reprehensible. My special one, Helen, winked her approval as she proffered Victor his plate. We went to the ballet—god knows where he found the money for tickets—

we went to the zoo. We walked around Boston Gardens and Beacon Hill.

For us, April was definitely not the cruelest month. I can't remember if the magnolias were in bud on Commonwealth and Marlborough, but they should have been. We sat in the darkest bar in Boston, in the old Lafayette Hotel, and nursed our drinks for hours at a time. I could make a sloe gin fizz, the only thing I could stand the taste of, last half the night.

"I'm going to marry you," my soldier said. "Come meet my family just in case, no strings attached, but I'm going to marry you." I seemed to have lost whatever mind of my own I had once had. We drove up to Salem to meet his sister, a child psychologist, and her pediatrician husband. I went to the train station to see Victor off, and he introduced me to his mother, who had also come to South Station to say her farewells. I was too shy to kiss her son good-bye in her presence. What a different world it was! His brother was at sea in the Pacific theater, a five-year stint, so meeting him would have to wait until the war's end. (At our wedding, Victor wore his brother's navy trousers. Two inches too short, two inches too big in the waist, they were the closest he could come to formal black attire. He also wore Jerry's black shoes, a size too big.)

There ensued a marathon of letter-writing. We wrote to each other daily for over a year, a ritual broken briefly in June when I traveled by train to Amarillo, Texas, and Victor hitchhiked down—across?—from New Mexico. I had an uncle in the air force who was stationed in Amarillo. His daughter, my childhood chum, had some sort of clerical position on the post, and I had come, it was announced, for a visit. After this I was to travel to Little Rock, Arkansas, where my lieutenant colonel brother and his wife had a new baby and needed any help they could get. My brother was finally stateside after going through the African campaign and the landing on the Italian boot. He had guarded Ger-

man POWs and stormed Monte Cassino but seemed dazed
by fatherhood. What I knew about baby-tending felt far
short of what I knew, for instance, about the Nicene Creed
or the Spenserian sonnet, but it was thought I could learn to
make myself useful.

Did my parents have any foreknowledge of this rendez-
vous in the Southwest? I think not. But my uncle, on learning that Victor and I could extend our two-day visit by
forty-eight hours if he went back to Los Alamos and signed
in, arranged for a hotel room in Albuquerque. This uncle
was on the lam from his marriage; he was having an affair
with a WAC captain. Clearly he thought all romantic desires deserved to be gratified. A free spirit, he had been an
underage sailor in the First World War. It is inexplicable
how he wormed his way as an officer into the Second and a
further mystery how he inveigled a hotel room in an over-
crowded town on a weekend full of military on overnight
passes.

We traveled to Alby by bus across the desert; the bus
broke down around midnight, and the passengers all disem-
barked to lie on the still-warm sand and admire the cactus
roses in bloom under a bright canopy of western sky. Following our sublime weekend in Albuquerque, Victor returned several hours late to the base and was rewarded with
a week's KP. I entrained for Little Rock and two weeks of
baby perambulation and housekeeping.

We didn't see each other again until Thanksgiving. In
what we now regarded as "our" bar of the Lafayette Hotel,
we agreed to become formally engaged and hastily arranged
a trip to Philadelphia so that Victor could meet my family.
"What would you do if I said no?" my father asked when he
asked for my hand. "I guess I'd marry her anyway," Victor replied. The engagement ring (chosen by my mother—I had
no interest in it) wiped out his savings. Twenty years later,
the diamond fell out of its setting somewhere on a bridle
path while I was snapping overhanging branches as we rode

along. I didn't notice the bare setting until that evening. Perhaps some millennia from now, its glint will catch the eye of a being who will take it back to the lair as an esoteric prize.

In December of that year, I elected to stay in Cambridge and work on my undergraduate honors thesis rather than go back to Philadelphia for the holidays. Rooms were made available at the Harvard Divinity School for those of us who had early (February) due dates for our magna opera. I had barely settled in to work when Victor arrived on an unexpected furlough. The water pipes at Los Alamos had frozen in an unprecedented cold snap, and the army had shipped several thousands of soldiers and scientists home until they could be repaired. What to do? I had a serious thesis to write.

Victor took charge. He came over each morning at eight with coffee and goodies and then absented himself all day. I read and scribbled diligently in my monk's cell, earning my release from drudgery on the dot of five, when Victor reappeared. On the stroke of midnight, he returned me to my appointed task. By the time our holiday together had ended, my thesis was nearly finished, reinforcing my already ingrained Jewish-Calvinist work ethic.

Just after my graduation in June of 1946, and a scant three weeks after he was mustered out of the army, Victor and I were married at the Warwick Hotel in Philadelphia in an elaborate ceremony staged entirely by my mother. It was to be a formal wedding, complete with *Lohengrin* and bridesmaids, unlimited champagne and platters of shrimp. We combed the city for a white dinner jacket to go with Victor's borrowed pants. Civilian clothes were all but unobtainable in that first postwar year, but he finally found a vintage number in Boston at Hirsch's Haberdashery on Massachusetts Avenue. I wore a satin bridal gown that had been worn before me by all three of my tiny sisters-in-law. A creative seamstress had altered it to fit me by changing the scoop neckline to an off-the-shoulder one and dropping the waist to hip height. I wore white ballet slippers; even so, the dress did not quite reach the desired floor length.

That elaborate charade behind us, we honeymooned in a borrowed farmhouse about twenty miles north of our own farm, a locus that became the inspiration for our move twenty-some years later to New Hampshire.

In the early days of the war, Victor had worked for a year and a half at the Woods Hole Oceanographic Institute conducting underwater explosions under the guidance of one of his Harvard professors. He had planned to go into the naval air force and said as much to E. Bright Wilson. "That's crazy!" Wilson exploded. "You'll be a dead hero. Come to Woods Hole and really help the war effort." But the army drafted him despite several high-level pleas to have him deferred. Sent off to undergo grueling basic training in the infantry, he was within days of being shipped overseas to fight in the Battle of the Bulge when he was snatched out of Alabama. Under sealed orders he was escorted to the train and eventually arrived at the Los Alamos facility. There, to his astonishment, he discovered a dozen former Woods Hole colleagues who had mysteriously disappeared one by one during his tenure, and at least one Harvard professor who had also gone missing the same way.

Because all military personnel were guaranteed reemployment at the last position held, we returned to Woods Hole after the war, where Victor had rented an apartment for thirty-five dollars a month in the old U.S. Bureau of Fisheries building. Seals barked outside our window. Waves lapped the pilings and lulled us to sleep. We had two rooms, one of which contained a sink, an ancient electric stove, and an icebox. The ice had to be replenished every other day, but the iceman never showed up on Mondays as he was sleeping off a hangover. On Mondays I rode my bike to the fish market and cadged a chunk of ice to bring home in my bike basket.

In his haste to find a place for us to live and his elation

over the reasonable rent, Victor had not noticed that the apartment lacked a bathroom. We shared a communal one with several bachelors up one flight and down a long outdoor corridor. I was the only woman in the building, but the dormitory-style bathroom was mine from nine till five. The rest of the time, Victor accompanied me and stood guard outside the door.

Except for the lack of our own indoor amenity, the apartment suited us perfectly. It was a great way to start off our marriage. Since I had little to do except learn how to iron shirts rather badly, I began to write in secret the poems I had abandoned when I matriculated at Radcliffe. Early in my freshman year I had submitted a batch of poems to a young instructor who was to become a famous novelist ten years later. He handed the sheaf back to me with a note at the top: "Say it with flowers, but for God's sake don't try to write poems about it." I was crushed. But creative writing was not held in high esteem at that time. Who knew that a thousand M.F.A. programs coast to coast were to come? It was felt that writing their own stories and poems deflected students from the serious business of accruing knowledge.

He was absolutely right about those early poems, a few lines of which come back to me:

> When lonely on an August night I lie
> Wide-eyed beneath the mysteries of space
> And watch unnumbered pricks of dew-starred sky
> Fearless drop past the earth with quiet grace . . .

Rhyme and meter alone do not a poet make.

In Woods Hole, Victor came home for lunch every day; his lab was literally within shouting distance. We swam or played tennis most evenings before supper and took the ferry to Martha's Vineyard frequently to spend weekends with various college friends whose families had cottages in Menemsha. Meat rationing was still in effect; we fished for many of our dinners. K. C.—Kung-Chi Wang—an engineer from MIT who was to marry one of my closest college chums, came down from his summer job in Providence quite regularly to play tennis and show us how to deal with the dozens of puffers we caught off the wharf. He filleted them expertly, extracting from the tail of this otherwise poisonous fish the one choice tidbit that he stir-fried in whiskey and soy sauce.

Those three months provided the carefree foreground our marriage needed. Once back in Boston, housing was expensive and hard to find. There were career decisions to make. After a few false starts, Victor signed on as a process engineer with Kendall Company in Walpole. Instead of atomic bombs, Kendall manufactured tampons and diapers. We moved six times that first year, from a one-roomer in the Back Bay to the top floor of what we later discovered was a fancy whorehouse in Brookline, and finally settled in one of those two-bedroom garden apartment housing developments that were mushrooming in rings around the big cities.

We were followed from place to place by the FBI, who interviewed our neighbors about our habits and practices and occasionally interviewed me on the pretext of inquiring about some unknown, nonexistent neighbor. David Greenglass had been in Victor's unit at Los Alamos; the Rosenberg case was about to blow open.

By then I had gone back to Harvard to earn my master's degree in comparative literature and quickly completed the required credits. Hugely pregnant with my first child, I flunked the Latin exam, for which I was underprepared. (The French exam was easy.) Harry Levin, who had been my tutor during my senior year, interceded for me on grounds of impending motherhood and prevailed on the committee to award the degree so long as I was not planning to go on for a Ph.D. Levin was a wonderfully generous mentor. He oversaw my undergraduate honors thesis, grandiloquently titled "Amorality and the Protagonist in the Novels of Stendhal and Dostoyevsky," and never flinched at the pretentiousness, gently steering me to various critical texts he thought I should read. Some ten years later, that M.A. enabled John Holmes to secure for me a profoundly underpaid and overworked adjunct teaching job at Tufts, my first venture into academia.

That halcyon year in graduate school I had another mentor, Albert Guerard Jr., who had, along with Mark Schorer and Otto Schoen-Rene, team-taught English I, a survey of English lit course I took as a freshman. Guerard conducted the most exciting graduate seminar of my brief academic career, a course John Simon, who went on to fame as a theater critic, was also enrolled in. I was high on Conrad, John on Gide, and all ten or twelve of us in the seminar were in Guerard's thrall, meeting ahead of time in the Hayes Bickford cafeteria to try out our literary theories and repairing there after class to continue the dialogue.

It didn't occur to me then to take note of the total absence of women faculty at Harvard. How myopic I was to complete four years as an undergrad, a fifth in grad school, blissfully unaware of their exclusion!

We had two babies in eighteen months and very little money. Most of our peers were in the same boat. The prevailing postwar temper cried out for stability, family, and a secure future. Most of us thought we wanted three, possibly four children, and we wanted to have them all close together so they could share their childhoods. We all read Dr. Spock religiously, who comforted us that we were probably doing things right without even knowing it.

Evenings and many weekends, Victor took over the child care as I researched various topics at the Boston Medical Library. Gradually I became a rather successful ghostwriter for a German psychiatrist whose sentences in English were impenetrable. I wrote papers for a surgeon doing experiments on burns, papers he then delivered at symposia as his own, and I ghosted for other physicians to whom my satisfied patrons referred me. Five dollars an hour was munificent pay. And while it wasn't exactly literary criticism, I was a freelance writer at last!

I don't think it occurred to us that we were in the vanguard in terms of marriage and parenting. Certainly it helped to be poor. We shared the household chores of laundry and marketing, folding diapers (we couldn't afford the then-burgeoning home diaper service, and besides, we got a lot of them free from Victor's workplace), amusing toddlers and sitting up with them through chicken pox and earaches. We read aloud to them and to each other, took them to free concerts on the Charles River in Boston and on day trips in the country.

We both had felt shortchanged in our childhoods; Victor's father had died, possibly a suicide, when Victor was five. His mother never quite got over her grief. She became a professional widow. And there were money problems during the ensuing Depression, problems that distracted her to the point where her youngsters received little more nurturing than food and shelter. Although I had grown up in a well-to-do household, my mother and I were at loggerheads. We could not please each other. She had, as she put it, "gone to the well four times" to get a daughter, but I was not the compliant female she had longed for. It was a cold relationship for my brothers as well. We kids were farmed out early, first to a nursemaid, then to day camps and overnight camps. I cannot remember a single family excursion other than the annual pilgrimage to Atlantic City to visit my father's mother. Victor and I were going to do a better job of parenting.

With three kids under the age of five, plus assorted household dogs and cats, every day was a challenge. The poetry never went away, however. I continued to write in the interstices of time between laundry and chauffeuring, between part-time medical editorial writing and part-time teaching of freshman composition at Tufts University. We bought a modest house in the suburbs. In 1963 we bought a derelict farm in New Hampshire.

Everyone grew up. The large children turned into interesting, even delightful, adults. We replaced them with horses, more dogs, and cats. We are still partners in possession of a long marriage, with too many horses, too ambitious a vegetable garden, too many sugar maple trees to tap. The family gathers in at Christmas and again in August. It's the way it should be, we think, and we are grateful for it.

CRUSHED OUT

PATRICIA CUMBIE

The things you notice about prospective lovers: his voice, smell, the hands. There's a cello sound to his voice; low, strong, no dramatic pitch. He's neat but not clean-cut, doesn't wear cologne. His scent is muffled and laundered. His fingers are long and thin, like mine. Bigger than what you'd expect for a person with such a small frame. We only touched that one time, and his hands were not so soft as I expected. The tips of his fingers are tough from playing stringed instruments. I think he bites his fingernails. The cuticles look a little rough. Still, I thought about them. What would his fingers do to a live body?

His hands are shaking. I see them searching for the security of a cigarette, something to do that restores normalcy. He's patting his shirt pockets. He's shit out of luck, and shows it. The gesture's a very adult thing for someone just this side of high school. I know the smokes are gone. I saw a crushed Camel box in his bag with the extra tapes he brought. He rubs his palms on his pants and exhales like a trapped animal. My hands are hangnail city. That's what I do when I'm agitated—pick at my fingers until they bleed. I wonder if he noticed that. I've nearly ripped my nails off altogether contemplating infidelity.

We are waiting for a pause in traffic, in clouds, for the lawn mower to quit humming in the background, because we're doing a work video together. We take a break and sit in his car—in a church parking lot, of all places. A poignant reminder of the sinful nature of humanity. I've fallen hard. Since he came back from film school to do this video project for me, I am surprised by how much I like him. I find myself throwing out workplace decorum, having too much fun encouraging his creativity and reckless inexperience. Over budget? That's okay. We'll work it out. It's what I want someone to do for me, encourage me to go overboard for the sake of art.

He's nearly half my age, quiet, serious, and seems equally susceptible to me. He's a respectful boy—mixed with potential—a future lady-killer. In the July heat, alone with him in the car, this is intoxicating. This crush is a feeling I've long forgotten, one I haven't felt since I was in the fourth grade, in line to go to the bathroom and in love with Tony Santucci. I can feel it "down there." This tingle, excitement that comes in waves while standing in line, looking at him, touching the marble wall of the hallway outside class to cool off. The marble smooth, a little cold pressing your cheek to it. I know I could crack my head open if I got pushed against it. It warms to my touch. My palms sweat on the marble. I add to it my breath. I draw little worlds on there through the moisture. Maybe there's Tony in there, a sun, a dog, a moon, and before you know it, it's my turn to go.

I'm afraid of what could happen next. We both look straight ahead, out the window of his car. Two crash dummies afraid to look at each other. I'm older, married. Kissing him is wrong.

The strange thing is, I am never really sure how tall he is. Once, during the filming of the video, I cracked a joke about being short, about liking "short guys," forgetting that maybe he isn't so tall. Like me, he's skinny and self-conscious about it. I like that about him. He looks the same all the time: Red Wing work boots, gray khaki pants, shirts in shades of falling leaves. He's definitely an Autumn. I tell him that.

"You're a perfect Autumn," I say. He looks at me, confused, but knows it has something to do with how he looks. He notices I notice how he looks.

"It has to do with the fact that your skin looks like it is lit from within, a sunset, sort of. And with those hazel eyes and blond hair, you look good in fall colors," I blabber on. "See, I'm a Winter. My skin is pale. I look good in red lipstick and black turtlenecks."

"Oh, I get it," he says, and turns away. I can tell by looking at the back of his neck, the way his head is tilted, that he is smiling.

There's something about being extensively photographed —no, filmed—that has me wired. I have never had the attention of one person trained on me for hours on end. I am a writer, not used to being someone else's subject, even for a work project. I think having a writer in your midst is like having a loaded gun in the house. You never know when it will go off, or who will end up getting shot. Normally, I'm the dangerous one, the one who will sniff out vulnerabilities on instinct. Right now I feel like I've just been bagged like a Canada goose during open season—stupid enough to get caught, dumb enough to think I wouldn't care. I did not know that I would like it too, and that a short video could hold out near-Faustian possibilities for my marriage. I am hell-bent on falling or flying with this guy.

All those Disney movies I watched as a kid come back to me, along with an adult sense and feminist shame. I have always wanted someone to look at me the way the prince looks at Cinderella/Sleeping Beauty/Snow White. I can't think of anyone who has ever gazed at me that way—but deep down, I've always been holding out for it. As a little girl, I thought that's what love must be like.

He's got me hooked to a microphone, the cord running

to a headset, says he can hear every little thing. He's patient. He waits more than anyone I can think of for a bit of quiet. My husband, on the other hand, hates to wait. He's a man in motion, gratified by active efficiency. He would never do one thing at a time. I admire how he does the work of three people effortlessly. But here I am, breathing in this calm young man. If he can hear everything through the mike, can he hear the sound of a heart switching loyalties? Him. Husband. Him. Hus . . .

So now I have a raging crush on a very young man because I believe in the possibility of Disney-love? I am married, I tell myself. I should have all my lines memorized, but I keep screwing up. This role is predetermined. Is it really so hard to stick to the script? He keeps smiling. I love my husband, but I am lusting for Mr. Video, wanting to hear more. I feel aroused, the vibrant part of my personality drawn out.

When he says, "Your hair is great," every time I complain about keeping my hair neat, I want to run away with him.

He has all the qualities of the perfect man: sensitive, artistic, and good-looking. I wish I were fifteen years younger. Or unmarried. That I had as much to show for my time on earth as this kid has—a body of work, awards, recognition.

He is kind about my mistakes, encouraging, sweet even. He always laughs when he says, "Okay, let's do it again."

Eventually pure exhaustion helps me relax. I am having fun creating this stupid little video. We joke about making a tape of my bloopers, but that's not the uncensored tape running through my mind.

"Okay," he signals with his right hand. Steers the camera with his left. A lefty. I start talking. I'm moving too much. Dammit. I'm mad at myself. Do it again. I start talking. I get it mostly right. It goes this way all day long. I try to shut him out, concentrate. When I look up, he is watching. It's his job, but I can't help but feel something. Is he looking for anything more? I hope he is, and I hope he isn't. The camera picks up every little thing.

When I watch the rough copy of the shoot, I'm shocked. I recall an interview I read in *Cosmo* about a professional model. She would conjure sexual fantasies while she worked, to make herself interesting to look at. Over the course of the day, on film I saw my pupils widen, my features relax. I'm lush, photogenic.

Is the young man's camera the window through which I have seen the future? That night, in the arms of my husband, I cry like I've not cried in years. We're in bed, the sheets crisp and clean, his touch a comfort. I am frightened, my body held in suspension because I am sobbing, but no tears. I am keening. But who died? His loving woman, the hopeful, naive one, has been replaced with someone willfully toying with temptation. How can I say, *I think I've found an artistic soul mate, and it's not you.*

I don't even know that I believe this, that how I feel is as high-toned as personal artistic freedom. But I wonder what it's like to have an artist for a lover, someone who is always engaged in the creative process. I fantasize about breakfasts where we could discuss the problems in our work—what to do with unwise characters, and how to resolve endings—then go off and fix them, fortified with symbiotic understanding and good advice. I'm guilty of thinking my husband's working-Joe self is not good enough for me. Are we good enough for each other? I don't know how to explain the void I feel between us, about my need to write. My crush has been a catalyst for understanding this ambition. I write but never talk about it.

I feel so vulnerable, I tell my husband. I tell him I am not a film professional. I screwed up so much. My husband, who can barely take centered pictures, let alone think about making feature films, suggests I "let it go."

Let it go, he whispers into my ear, running a finger through my hair. Posterity won't be harmed by your actions.

My crush is getting to be a problem of tabloid proportions. Now that Mr. Crush has gone back to school, I think I'd like to surprise him and run off to New York, be the seductive older woman, maybe start chain-smoking. I want to do something truly destructive rather than feel crushed whole and canned. I would rather go through experiences like a spirit and vanish, no consequences. Facing the truth has been too painful: I'd like to be completely immersed in a writerly existence, ditching my husband to be sexually charged by some young thing. I don't want the life I have in a fixer-upper house in the city, a dog, a job, a cat, a car, the regular mealtimes.

For weeks I think about this. I am under the influence of some intimate pressure, the video having turned my mind here and there. I imagine myself in new scenarios, each one more removed from present reality than the other. I am driven to distraction with the force of suppressed creativity. Desire to be more is weighting the rest of my life. I am again and again in front of the camera, driven by a lust to be perfect, seductive, brighter than before. This is the place and time I go for it, the will bending practical resistance: *I will go through with it.*

Or I am behind the camera, telling him where to move, using that same voice—a deliberate calling of his name that causes him to soften like a baked apple. I direct his movement until it curls his cerebrum, treading away the leaves in his hair, stripping the ego. He is my muse, and I am creating him, jotting him down in hard ink on postcards of foreign mountains, rivers, forests. He is put down where I want him to be—behind the scenes of every powerful moment. The power of change is settled on this picture; in this story each frame is imperceptibly different. I am pursuing my love, my passion. I feel sluggish, licked, and warm through and through. I can live this way if I choose.

My husband: reliable, persistent, permanent. He's a Winter too. Black Irish. Blue eyes, dark hair, a smattering of gray. The type I'm usually attracted to, not a golden boy. Right now he is doing what you'd call "working on our marriage." Of course he doesn't say this. I know it. He's clued in to the crush somehow. It's these kinds of questions:

"So you're bored with our lovemaking? Is there anything you'd like me to do different?"

He asks at the right time. We're not fighting about sex, dishes, time together, money. I tell him no, not really.

Just your penchant for watching women with big breasts, liking lacy bras too much, your Buddha belly, your wishing I were someone I'm not—goes mercifully unsaid. I'm feeling defensive already. The jig is up. I'm bored off my ass with this life of ours.

If I feel creative frustration, or lust for another person, my husband's not to blame, is he? If I want something, I should be able to articulate it. But could he be a film student from New York for a while? Help me get over this thing? Would he mind believing I am the most interesting woman in the world? Would my husband mind being someone he's not?

No, not really. That pisses him off. I always say that.

But I'm thinking—a person shouldn't always know what her lover is thinking. Is this crush really hurting my marriage? A magazine survey I read in *Ladies Home Journal* (now there's an authority) claimed that people—like me—who have secret thoughts are a bad marriage risk. And what writer doesn't? But I'm starting to see that my relationship to my writing and to my husband is bound up in a jealous, loverlike competition, and I automatically believe he won't understand. We could have a meeting of minds, but we will crave two different things in a relationship. He love. She art.

I decide to meet Mr. Crush for lunch when he's home for Christmas break because I need a hit of the drug that's kept me going since July. We go to a café in a tony suburb near his parents' house. It's the kind of café where you can get a salad with vinaigrette that costs more than an honest hour's wage. The frisée on my plate of mixed greens is out of hand. It's curling all over; the spiky yellow edges menace, and they don't go too delicately into the mouth. I open wider to shove them in. Too much endive too. The French soup is al dente. This is not date food. I tell myself, this is not a date.

I didn't tell anyone I was meeting him. It's not like I need to pretend I am not meeting him. Still, I feel like I need to keep quiet. When feelings are that close to the exterior, you automatically protect them. When does a sympathetic friend turn into two hands with calluses, an amiable mouth, a downy neck—in short, someone you want to sleep with?

We chitchat. The small stuff. New York hip vs. Minnesota nice. He looks in my eyes when he speaks. Laughs sincerely. I swear he's still got that Autumn halo. I've been thinking this potential sort-of-thing with this young filmmaker is real chemistry. What if the story goes differently for him? What if the story goes, *She's not bad, I wouldn't mind it with her, but not if it's too much work. She's married, for chrissake.*

My husband and I decide we really need to do something different. We try new positions, sexy undies, wine, but nothing changes. Every time we make love, the bed squeaks. Just like in the movies, you're cued to know something's happening in the next room. The voyeur in a person gets aroused. Whenever I get on top of him it starts, like some dog toy. At first it's amusing. You crack a smile—*you know what they are up to.*

But it's indicative of something out of repair, the habit too resolute to change. I am doing what I'm always doing, getting on top of him, his hands on my hips, my breath in his ear. He is not transported by ecstasy, nor am I. This noise is not sexy. This is Pavlovian: The bed is squeaking, he is almost ready. The bed is squeaking, he is distracted and so am I. The bed is squeaking, squeaking, squeaking. Finally it stops.

I am emboldened by secrecy. The vacuum sound in the café is a slushy counterpoint to staccato desire. I didn't tell anyone I was going to see him, so whatever happens, nobody but us will know. This moment is squared in time. A slice off the old filmmaker's block never to see the light of day.

"I've been writing about you," I tell him. "Nothing bad," I blurt.

Do I mean the quality of the writing is good, or that he'd be flattered by the attention? Or is this bad for him that I even mention that I've sort of turned the tables on him? Still, I worry, like I worry for my husband, that I will hurt him. Maybe he's too inexperienced for this. His mother would freak. I can feel her mind flip: "Older-woman-writes-story-about-seducing-my-son."

He doesn't squirm. He actually doesn't say anything. I keep going.

"Being observant is the artist's gift." I am speaking platitudes. I can't stand myself when I get like this. I'm a terrible seductress.

He nods. He knows what I mean. Really.

"It's a gift and, and a curse." You can only get away with saying this sort of stuff in a café while cappuccino froth is being made in the background.

"I had this silly dream. That we went to the prom. I guess it's because you're young, and in real life I never went."

As soon as I said it, I wished I hadn't. Why am I always longing for romantic events that never materialize? I am so pathetic.

"Yeah, I didn't go either. I couldn't get into it," he says. Of course. He's got loftier ambitions than being a prom king.

In the dream I wore a silver dress with sequins and no underwear. "In this dream we kiss." I hesitate for a moment. A zing hits my palms, remembering what it felt like in my dream.

I woke up wet, sweating, my flannel nightie twisted up around my waist. My husband half a bed away from me.

"Anyway, I'm writing about the fact that I have, well, a crush on you. I felt like I needed to tell you, before you found out about it, or something, somewhere."

I touch his hand. It's warm. Mine are freezing.

"Cold hands, warm heart," he oh-so-eloquently points out.

I just put it out there, and that's all he can say. What do I expect? The Cinderella treatment? Suddenly I feel like I have to go. To the bathroom. I'm in there—disappointed, ashamed—ready to throw the tastefully hand-painted container of soft soap against the wall.

I don't want him.

I want what he has. Freedom. A trust fund. My heart.

I go home and discover our bed in pieces. The whole thing has been dismantled, and like the scarecrow in *The Wizard of Oz,* it's all over the room. The bedding is in a pile. The mattress smothers the bed pillows. The frame is here and there, against the wall and zig-zagged across the room. It looks like the work of some psycho.

I did not expect such swift retribution for sneaking off.

My husband appears in the middle of it all, vacuum nozzle in hand. He looks like a domestic at a cheap hotel, dressed in sweat pants, no shirt. His prominent chest hairs curl over the line of good taste.

I'm happy to see him.

"You wouldn't believe what a mess was under here," he says, pushing his glasses up on his nose. "At least ten pounds of cat hair. While you were gone, I've been tightening the screws. All of them. A lot of them were loose. I'm sure they were causing our squeaking problem."

"So you were screwing, eh?"

"Yeah," he says. "You wanna help me put this thing back together?"

II

Changing Terrain

Close your eyes and it comes,

the music of old roads . . .

—Linda Hogan

AN OUTING WITH ISABELLE

JOAN ARCARI

I lied about my age. Also about having three kids waiting at home when I finally got there. Some nights I hung out with my friends in Greenwich Village until three in the morning. Then I'd wake up the next day and bake cookies with my kids. Yes. But no one in my Village life knew that. I didn't really lie. I learned to make good conversation like playing chess. Deft maneuvering; obfuscation. There were things I didn't talk about: the kids, the house in the suburbs, the uncooperative ex-husband.

I'd scare the men right back into the trees if I did, my psychotherapist brother-in-law warned me. I protested in a wave of feminist consciousness. (It was the time for that.) And he said, "Of course it shouldn't be that way. It just is." I decided he was probably right.

It was the right thing to do on the job market, too. Even if they knew you had a family and it was cool because they were equal opportunity types, they'd ask you to make cookies for the Christmas party instead of promoting you. Don't-ask-don't-tell was just the best way all around.

It didn't take long for me to get to be the woman who was different from the other women in my crowd. I didn't gossip; I didn't personalize. Not on your life! My discussions were theoretical. Most of the men I talked to were easy that way. They never asked anyway. If you had wanted them to know about your personal life, you would have had to squeeze it in while they took a breath.

Joe and I were talking one night. Probably about politics—about which candidate was going to do the best job cleaning up the city. He knew. He had connections at city hall. One of the women we knew was up for city court judge. I liked her because she was a regular person.

"She's just a housewife!" Joe said, waving her away just like that.

I never said a word. I never came to her defense, never asked how being a housewife would disqualify her for the job. Or even exactly what he meant. We were treading in precarious territory. In fact, I was flattered that I was so far from the housewife category that Joe felt free to say it. On some level, I felt like a success. At obfuscation. I used to worry that I would make it so big, I'd have to give my secrets away. It never became a problem.

Technically speaking, of course, I wasn't a housewife. Except for being married to a house. An old house in the country with three kids. What I was, was a traitor.

"Who do we say we are if it's one of your city friends calling?" my son would ask. He meant a guy, of course. Women aren't so easily fooled.

Kids grow up. They got to be twenty-one, twenty-two, and I got to be forty and more, which is when I had planned to jump off a bridge. But I wasn't ready to do that. Instead, I tried not to think about it.

"You going to lie about our age now, too, Mom?" the kids, no longer kids, asked. I wasn't fooling them.

A few years later, Joe married a woman in our crowd. She seemed a lot younger, but I didn't know Joe's age or hers. I never asked. As I said, age was not a topic of my conversations. She was pregnant. It was trendy to be pregnant. I had already done that—starting about thirty years before when it wasn't trendy and I'd never heard of a biological clock.

Joe and his new wife almost dropped out of sight. Ru- ̄they'd bought a house in the suburbs somewhere. ̄'d come in from time to time. Mostly we talked about the usual: city politics. His wife came in when the old hangout closed down and there was a farewell party. By that time I didn't have the house in the suburbs anymore. I was living alone now. I didn't have a husband or a house or kids at home. I was an honest woman. Almost.

When men like Joe said, "I can't believe you were ever married," I was still flattered.

The truth? I was married and pregnant before I knew what hit me, before I had an identity, or, at least, the strength to assert it. I had been a kid and I had three kids while I was still in my early twenties, and I was divorced shortly after I was thirty. So now I was living a belated single life, the one I never got to live before.

When one of my daughters decided to get married, I asked her why she wanted to do that. "Why not just go on living together?"

"Mom, most mothers are happy that their daughter's going to marry a handsome lawyer."

It wasn't that I was an anarchist or anything like that. It's just that having a married kid is harder to hide—especially when they decide to live in the Village. It meant I had four kids now. It meant I was really grown up, even middle-aged.

After the wedding, however, I felt a bit liberated. I went so far as to have a few pictures around that I'd forget to cover up when I entertained.

"Is that your sister? She looks like you."

"It's my daughter."

"You didn't tell me you had a grown daughter," said a brand-new man in my life.

"I'm telling you now."

"You don't look old enough to have grown-up kids."

"I'm not." Period. It was a beginning. And usually an end as well. There still wasn't a whole lot of interest in such things among my friends. Which saved me.

I made a discovery: The kids aren't as threatening when they don't live at home. Who did I think I was kidding in

terms of age, anyway? I didn't dye my hair, didn't have colla-
gen treatments. When I hit fifty, I still didn't jump off a
bridge. In fact, it was better than forty.

One of my daughters became mildly famous. I was torn
between boastful maternal pride and my usual familial reticence. I boasted.

Then the married daughter got pregnant. She didn't
know how I was going to take it. Not after the way I took to
her getting married. "I'm no kid, after all, Mom," she explained. Biological clock again. Contrary to what everyone
expected, I was delighted when she told me. How do you
know how you're going to react to anything until it
happens?

Isabelle was born. My apartment and my desk at work
were filled with pictures of her at every developmental
stage. All anyone had to do was ask to see the latest baby pictures. I'd forget whatever antiestablishment tack I was on
and whip them right out of my knapsack. Sometimes I
didn't wait to be asked. I can only imagine what they said behind my back: How boring?

It's a beautiful sunny Saturday, and I'm pushing Isabelle
down Bleecker Street. "We'll get some bread at Zito's," I tell
her. I keep the stroller seat facing me so I can talk to her. I
don't think I've ever felt happier—more complete—in my
life. Isabelle smiles up at me. She makes steady talking
sounds that aren't quite words yet, and I smile back and
make sounds that are not quite my normal voice. "Are you
Gram's little girl?" Embarrassing. This is Bleecker Street, after all. Almost the center of my world. People bustle past us
on the crowded sidewalk while I unashamedly stop the
stroller and lean over to kiss Gram's baby's chubby cheeks.

A familiar man stops, stone still, and turns sideways to
into the stroller. "And who is this?" he asks, bending
e.

I flash him a smile as large and bright as Isabelle's. "My granddaughter," I say, proudly biting the bullet. I have been outed right here on Bleecker Street.

"Oh yeah?" he says. "I didn't know you had grandchildren." He leans over, smiles, and reaches out his hand to Isabelle. She makes a fist around his pinky and pulls it to her mouth. "Aren't they great? I've got three."

"Really? I didn't know that."

"From my first marriage." He moves closer to let people pass by. "You know what I say? If I'd known grandchildren were so good, I'd have had them first."

"I agree. Absolutely."

We walk along Bleecker Street swapping notes and gossip like old times. Almost.

BOILED CHICKEN FEET
AND HUNDRED-YEAR-OLD EGGS

POOR CHINESE FEASTING

S H I R L E Y   G E O K - L I N   L I M

"You mustn't eat chicken feet until you are a married woman!" my aunts warned me. "Otherwise you will grow up to run away from your husband."

They sat around the dining table, an unstable jointure of old planks stained by years of soy-sauce drips and scorched by the ashy embers that always fell out of the small coal oven under the metal hot pot which was fetched out once a year for Chinese New Year family feasts. They chewed on gold-brown chicken feet that had been boiled with ginger, garlic, sugar, and black soy. The feet looked like skinny elegant batons with starred horny toes at one end, their speckled skins glossy with caramelized color, but chicken feet all the same. My aunts and stepmother gnawed at the small bones, grinding the jellied cartilage of the ligaments audibly, and the bone splinters piled up beside their plates.

I would not stay to watch them. I had seen hens and roosters pick their feet through fungal monsoon mud, stepping on duck and dog and their own shit.

My stepmother raised poultry on our leftovers and on chopped swamp vegetation which sprouted lavishly in the greenish slimy wasteland behind our house, and on festival days she slaughtered at least two fat chickens for us—her five stepchildren, two sons, and cherished husband. Chicken was a luxury we tasted only on those days, on Chinese New Year, Ch'ing Ming, the Mid-Autumn Festival, and the Feast of the Hungry Ghost. And then, as my aunts told us was the practice even when they were children, the chickens were divided according to gender, the father receiving the white breast meat, the sons the dark drumsticks, and the daughters the skinny backs, while the women ate the feet and wings.

As the only daughter in a family (then) of seven boys, I was excused from such discrimination and took my turn equally with the drumsticks, the favorite meat for all of us. Chicken was always sold whole and freshly slaughtered, and no one imagined then that one could make a dish solely of drumsticks or of chicken breasts. Such mass marketing was possible only with the advent of refrigeration, and although coffee shops in town held large industrial-sized refrigerators for serving shaved iced concoctions and cold sodas, popular refreshments among Malaysians to fend off the humid equatorial temperatures, Chinese Malaysians, like most Asians in the 1950s, would eat only fresh food. We thought of frozen meat as rotten, all firm warm scented goodness of the freshly killed and gathered gone, and in its place the monochromatic bland mush of thawed stuff fit only for the garbage pail.

Still, while no one sold chicken parts separately, fresh chicken feet were always available in the wet market; you could buy them by the kilo, a delicacy to be enjoyed, according to my elders, only by married women. Well, let my aunts and stepmother suck on those splintery bones. I was never comfortable at the table when those feet appeared, when the women waved me away from them. My mother had run away from her husband. A bad woman, a runaway wife, a lost mother. A young girl, I was not to be trusted with those chicken feet, not when I had my mother's history in my blood, my mother's face on my face, still recognizable to my aunts, my father's brothers' wives, good wives and mothers, even though it had been five, six, seven years since she ran away.

I could not face the leathery skin, tightly bound to the long femurs after hours of simmering. And the soft padded soles that my aunts delighted in chewing—it was here that the chicken came closest to the human anatomy: pads like the fat feet of my stepmother's babies. Even now, now that I have grown to become a wife and mother like my aunts and stepmother, like my runaway mother, I will not eat chicken feet, no matter how much wine, cardamom, cumin, honey, or ginger has steeped them. I remember the tiny bones, the crunch of skin and cartilage. I remember my mother.

Almost forty years later, living in the United States, I am constantly reminded of how "Chinese" has become a fetish for Americans looking for a transcending experience of difference and otherness. Ranging from white models with stark black eyeliner and chopsticks in their chignons to "happy" dressing gowns that copy karate-type uniforms, things associated with Chinese culture pervade mainstream American imagination, suggesting, through the fixed acquirement of a traditional middle-class taste—for the blue willow-pattern china, for instance, or take-out shrimp in lobster sauce—that Americans are omnivorous consumers rather than Eurocentric ideologues.

Purveyors of such U.S. "multiculturalism," however, usually disguise the material sources of their goods. Difference has to be softened, transformed, before it can be assimilated into Middle America. So also with Chinese food, which, before Nixon's visit to China in 1972, was sold in thousands of small restaurants outside of Chinatowns as egg rolls, egg foo yung, chow mein, and fortune cookies, none of which was recognizable to me who had grown up eating home-cooked Chinese food in Malaysia. Influenced by the increase in Asian immigration to the United States after the 1965 Hart-Celler Act, and thirty years after Mao Tse-tung intoxicated the Nixon presidential party with *maotai* and exotic ten-course banquets, many Americans have learned to dine on "authentic" Chinese food across a number of regional cuisines, from the mild, flavorful fresh steamed dishes of Canton, to the salty fiery peppers of Szechwan and Hunan and the rich elaborate foods of the Shanghainese. But mid-Manhattan restaurants and Chinese cookbooks never note the particular dishes peculiar to Old One-Hundred-Name, what the Chinese call the man on the street. These dishes have been the ordinary fare for billions of poor Chinese through the centuries, and for myself as a hungry child in a family of too many children and never enough money.

While the chicken feet my aunts feasted on were forbidden to me, I was repeatedly coaxed to taste *pei ta-an*, the only other dish in my famished childhood that I could not eat. These duck eggs, imported from China, had been selected for their large size, covered with a mix of mud and straw, then stored in a darkened space for at least a month, covered with cloth that had been impregnated with sodium carbonate. You had to knock the dried gray mantle of mud gently off, wash the eggs in cold water, then crack and peel the bluish-white shells. What emerged was a clear glistening gelatinous black oval enclosing a purple-green-black yolk, and a sharp reek of sulfuric vapor, a dense collection of chemicals from decaying things, like the airborne chemical traces that trigger the salivary glands of scavenging wolves or turkey buzzards.

Father was especially fond of *pei ta-an,* what the expensive restaurants called hundred-year-old eggs, which my stepmother always served sliced thin in sections of eighths accompanied by shredded pink young ginger pickled in sugared vinegar. He believed it was *poh,* full of medicinal properties that stimulated blood circulation, cleansed the liver and kidneys, sharpened the eyesight and hearing, and elevated the male libido, and my stepmother, a generation younger than he, diligently served it as a cold relish to accompany steaming rice porridge, or alone, as a late-night snack.

Occasionally Father shared this delicacy with us. My brothers hung greedily over him, waiting for their one-eighth sliver of slippery shining jet-black egg, which was served draped with a vinegary-moist ginger shred. Approaching *pei ta-an* for the first time, I thought its glistening black carapace and iridescent green-black yolk beautiful, a magical gem cut open for inspection. But then its acrid stench shot up my olfactory glands, opening passageways more powerfully than a tongueful of green mustard, and I gagged, as close to vomiting over food as I would ever get. Unlike boiled chicken feet, which I could ignore by resolutely leaving the table, *pei ta-an* pursued me out of the kitchen, out of the living area, and out of the house, a smell of pollution I feared each time Father called out for us to come and eat some hundred-year-old egg.

At some point in my childhood, however, drawn by my brothers' lust for *pei ta-an*, I pinched my nostrils closed and opened my mouth for the sliver. Its flavor and texture were like nothing I had ever tasted, the combination of the jellied white-turned-to-black and the tightly packed purple-black heart igniting on my taste buds as an intricate instantaneous sensation of bitter and sweet, rawly and densely meaty, yet as delicate as air-spun cotton candy, primitively chemical and ineffably original. I was hooked. But *pei ta-an*, although not expensive, was what my stepmother bought for Father alone: for his health, his pleasure, his libido. A morsel would always be our share of this pleasure.

Late on the evening that I first tasted *pei ta-an* I walked out to the Chinese grocery store at the corner of the main road and spent some of my cache of coins hoarded from the dollars that my mother far away in another country mailed me once or twice a year. I bought two eggs jacketed in mud and straw. While my brothers were playing Monopoly in the front room, I sneaked into the kitchen, broke open the armor, carefully crazy-cracked the shells, peeled the pair, all the time marveling at the scent that had set my saliva flowing, and ate them slowly, reveling in the gentle chewy texture of the albumen and the heavy metallic yolky overload. My stepmother was right. Eating *pei ta-an* was a libidinous experience.

I have grown accustomed to the absence of strong flavor and scent in food, living in the United States. Many Americans appear to prefer their meals as antiseptic as their bathrooms. The movement toward "health foods" seems to me to be yet another progression toward banning the reek, bloodiness, and decay of our scavenging past and installing a technologically controlled and scientifically scrutinized diet. In some future time, humans may live to 150 years, dining on a mass-produced nutritious cuisine of "natural foods" based on grains, vegetables, and roots. Boiled chicken feet and chemically preserved eggs will become gross memories from a horrible history of animal abuse and carcinogenic poisoning. But in the meantime, millions of Asians are still eating these dishes in search of, if not, as my poor father who died young of throat cancer believed, health and longevity, at least a diverse diet that can keep them body and soul.

Thus my eldest brother, by now middle-aged and middle-class prospering, promised me a memorable breakfast when I visited him in Malacca in 1989. It was a Sunday, as in the West a day for leisurely gatherings and perhaps some family feasting. We drove to the center of town, up through a narrow side-lane, and parked by an open ditch. Under a galvanized tin roof, crowding with other families, we sat on low stools around a small round wooden table, as scarred and stained as the table around which we ate in our childhood. The hawker, a Chinese Malaysian, was busy stirring an enormous blackened iron pot from which clouds of steam puffed up. Smaller pots containing various dark and green mashes sat on smaller grills, all fueled by a propane tank. Pouring the boiling liquid from the teapot, Eldest Brother rinsed the bowls, cups, spoons, and chopsticks set before us. Then a woman—the hawker's wife? daughter?—filled our bowls with plain white rice porridge, watery, the grains soft but still separate rather than broken down into a glutinous mass. From the many pots she brought different bowls— salted cabbage cooked to a dark-green slush with slabs of pork fat edged with a little lean; salted pickled cucumber crunchy and sweet; hard-cooked and browned bean curd less chewy than the meat it was processed to imitate; salted dried anchovies smaller than my little finger, fried crisp with their heads on. Nothing was fresh, everything was freshly cooked.

A light in my head flashed and lit something I had always known but never understood. How poor the masses of ordinary Chinese have been for millennia and how inventive hunger has made them. How from the scraps, offal, detritus, and leftovers saved from the imperial maw, from dynastic overlords who taxed away almost everything, peasant Chinese have created a fragrant and mouthwatering survival: dried lily buds and lotus roots, tree cloud fungus and fermented bean mash, dried lichen and salted black beans, pickled leeks and seaweed dessert, fish maw and chicken feet, intestines and preserved eggs. No wonder as a child I was taught to greet my elders politely, "Have you eaten yet, Eldest Auntie? Have you eaten rice, Third Uncle?" Speaking in our dialect, my stepmother still greets me, newly arrived from rich America, thus, "Have you eaten?"

The cook himself approached our table bearing two dishes especially ordered by my brother for me: soy-boiled chicken feet chopped into bite-sized pieces, and *pei ta-an* cut in eighths with a mound of pickled ginger on the side. My eldest brother had figured me out; that, even after decades of American fast foods and the rich diet of the middle class, my deprived childhood had indelibly fixed as gastronomic fantasies those dishes impoverished Chinese had produced out of the paltry ingredients they could afford. This is perhaps the instruction to an increasingly consuming and consumed planet that the cuisine from China offers: To eat is to live. And we multiplicious billions will all have to learn to eat well in poverty, turning scarcity and parsimony to triumphant feasting. Facing my morning's breakfast of preserved vegetables and hundred-year-old eggs, boiled chicken feet, and rice gruel, I knew my brother was offering me the best of our childhood together.

DIANA ANHALT

I write about my childhood for the same reason some people visit cemeteries: to come to terms with the past and let my dead know I forgive them. Perhaps I hope to strike a bargain with my mother and father. "Look, I'll write about what happened and try to explain, but only if you promise to behave and stop flapping about in my head like sheets in the wind."

Toward the end of her life, my mother, Belle, told me, "If you don't understand something, write about it." I'd like to believe she was giving me permission to explore their closely guarded pasts. Then I could get on with my own life.

On October 22, 1950, the day before we vanished from the Bronx, Belle and Mike casually mentioned to my younger sister, Judy, and me as we finished lunch, "We're going to California, kids, just a short trip, we promise. Take two toys each, nothing bulky." Indulging me, they allowed me to take my ice skates, provided I would carry them. I knotted the laces together and wore them around my neck.

"This was my first plane trip and I wasn't convinced—all evidence to the contrary—that man could or should fly," my mother wrote in her journal. *"We landed in Dallas in a blinding downpour—just the sort of crummy weather you'd expect in Texas. Here, we were delayed for several hours. Engine trouble. I reminded Mike how I'd wanted to take the train. But the decision had already been made. Now it was fly or stay in Texas. I flew."*

Handing out chewing gum and chatting with passengers, an American Airlines Junior Stewardess pin fastened to my chest, I followed the airline hostess down the aisle. A passenger glanced up from her knitting to ask, "Where are you going, dear?"

"To California," I replied.

"Well, if you're going to California, you're on the wrong plane because this one is going to Mexico."

I trotted back up the aisle to tell my parents just in case they didn't know. "What! We didn't tell you we were going to Mexico? Well, it doesn't matter. California and Mexico are neighbors, you know."

Since they seemed unconcerned, and the stewardess needed my help, I forgot the incident. Not until years later would I discover that my small mother, moving through rooms like a brisk wind in her tweeds and sensible pumps, and my father, handsome, irreverent, and dogmatic—someone people listened to and everyone, except possibly my mother, feared—were probably running from the law. During the '50s, the McCarthy era, my parents' active participation in left-wing politics and possible membership in the Communist Party could have unpleasant consequences. For them and scores of others, fleeing America was a viable alternative to receiving a subpoena, losing a job, or, in the worst of cases, going to jail. At the time, however, I was convinced our abrupt departure for Mexico City was merely one more attempt to make my life miserable.

The day we left, I was to be the apple blossom in the school festival. A week earlier, I'd purchased pink crepe paper for my costume and cut, gathered, and stapled it together in four layers so my tutu would stand straight out. All the way to the airport I repeated, "Mrs. Leoffler will never forgive me. I promised, I promised." And when I closed my eyes, I could almost hear my fourth-grade teacher announcing through the megaphone, "Well, wouldn't you know?

Diana Zykofsky, the same little girl who wet her pants going down the sliding pond last month, didn't even bother to come. And she had the part of the apple blossom!"

Years after, I would dream I was still eight years old, sitting at the kitchen window in our Bronx apartment, waving good-bye to my sister and myself as we were borne away in the back seat of my Uncle Aaron's dark blue Studebaker. We sped down a highway divided by a yellow line, then screeched dramatically to a stop at the rim of a precipice— the border.

The dream highway was the same one coiling its way through the travel posters. During one of its periodic publicity campaigns, the Mexican tourism department distributed a poster to travel agencies with a map of Mexico and the United States, through which wound a road with a yellow line down the middle. This was superimposed on a serape-striped background against which two hands—one coffee colored, one pink—stood out in sharp relief, reaching in a clasp across the border, represented by a heavy black line snaking from one side of the map to the other.

I marveled at how easy the poster made the gap between countries appear and wondered whether it would, in fact, be possible to pinpoint the exact place where the United States ended and Mexico began. What if a volcano erupted at the point where the countries met? (Before we arrived, a volcano called Paricutín had risen like warm dough out of a farmer's cornfield, swelling to engulf the neighboring farms.) Were that to happen, how would they know with certainty where the real border was?

Before going to Mexico, the farthest I'd been from home was Camp Kinderland in Hopewell Junction, New York. A three-hour drive in Sunday morning traffic, it lay continents away from the Bronx, and my memories of it are bathed in yellow and smell like pancakes—even the lake, shimmery along its reed-covered edges, hard and dull as rock toward the center. Shivering, we'd line up at the pier's edge. I'd grasp my water buddy's wrist and she mine. When the blast of the counselor's whistle pierced our eardrums, deadening the drone of mosquitoes, we'd plunge into the lake. Rushing up through the surface as if launched for take-off, I saw flashes of silver, purple, and green, and at this precise moment, I was the farthest I'd ever been from the Bronx.

Yet nothing, not even that, prepared me for Mexico. When we stepped out the side entrance of Shirley's Courts Motel the day after our arrival, I saw real palm trees for the first time, and the realization of how far we had come hit me with an intensity, almost physical, like electric shocks. Everything vied for my attention: the blasts of color—chartreuse, magenta, orange, and yellow—and the smells, an astringent chalkiness I would later recognize as corn dough, the harsh bitterness of toasting chilies, cinnamon. Beggars waved mutilated limbs in front of my face. Stray dogs sniffed my crotch.

Even the familiar things were painful. I remember walking past a Jewish delicatessen. Inhaling the pungent smell of pickles and smoked mackerel, I was reminded of my grandmother and home and had to bite down hard on my lower lip to keep from crying.

Before long it grew obvious that the short trip my parents had promised was turning into something else. Within a few months, Belle was working as a legal secretary in an American law firm, and my father rented space in a flower shop on Avenida Juárez where he sold the lamps he made out of colonial statuettes and pre-Columbian pots purchased in small towns and markets. His merchandise also included ex-votos or *milagros* (miracles). Crudely painted on pieces of tin salvaged from flattened-out cans, the offerings thanked God for impregnating the sterile, restoring sight to the blind, reviving the dead, and providing safe harbor for the living.

By then we had met a few other families who arrived in

Mexico as precipitously as we. Sunday afternoons we spent at each other's houses eating barbecued hamburgers or enchiladas and rice and listening to jazz recordings or Burl Ives and the Weavers' folk songs. The adults waved their arms a lot and spoke loudly as they discussed Korea or "that bastard McCarthy." But as soon as the Rosenbergs' anticipated executions were mentioned, they lowered their voices or passed on to a lighter topic: how long to boil the milk, where to buy the *New York Times*, who intended to return to the States.

Belle and Mike stayed thirty years. Today, I alone remain in Mexico to remind my brother and sister of Agustina, the cook, who took care of us, taught us the words to *"Adiós Mariquita Linda"* and how to whistle through our teeth. Without me, they would forget how to eat chilies and drink tequila, to roll their *r*'s like natives and their tortillas so the sauce won't ooze out, to dance a *danzón*, curse in Spanish, and drive in Mexico City.

After they left, I seriously considered painting a *milagro* like the ones my father sold in his store. Mexico's Virgin of Guadalupe would appear on one side, and my Uncle Benny, who set up my parents in the TV sales distribution business and turned them into capitalists, on the other. Under crossed flags, one Mexican, one American, float Belle and Mike, the two Jewish radicals. I would paint my sister and myself raising our baby brother, Paul, born in Mexico, high above our heads. He waves a banner bearing the words *Viva México.* Such memories must never be lost.

I never painted that *milagro,* but after my parents' deaths, I started to write in search of answers: Who am I? Where does the old me end and the new me begin? Where are my borders? Understanding, the longest journey of all, seeps in slowly, not through my brain but rather through my fingertips, like Braille, and clings to my skin like sand.

WHAT IT MEANS TO STAY

Margaret Lynn Brown

The flotsam and jetsam of my love life lay heaped on the driveway. My Welsh terrier, Kishke, looked doubtful about it all piling into a four-door Dodge Colt. Although my sister now had a closet full of boxes, elsewhere in Minneapolis that night there would be a truly blessed Dumpster digger.

As we set sail the next morning on I-94, Kishke, the bulging Colt, and I joined previous generations of emigrants and prairie schooners. My maternal grandparents left Sweden for America the year the *Lusitania* sank. My father's people left North Carolina after the War of 1812 to find better land, and succeeding generations scattered the Great Plains from Minnesota to Oklahoma and Colorado, as if caught in a blast of the Dust Bowl. Although I had lived most of my then twenty-eight years in Minnesota, you might say that rootlessness was a family tradition.

That morning, however, the frontier stretched southeast, toward North Carolina. I hoped to have an adventure, maybe find the top of ole Smoky, before settling down to graduate school applications. And of course, I lived in a world kinder to single women than any of my pioneer ancestors might imagine. Still, I had somehow lost my moorings with the change of my last name, and it felt good to be driving away.

That first afternoon in the Effigy Mound National Monument, we saw the shapes of marching bears created out of earth by ancient hands. Barely into Iowa, it already seemed like something just might happen. In Dubuque we ate corn dogs; in Hannibal, Huck Finn burgers. By the time we got to Memphis we hadn't seen one family that reminded me of the one I no longer had. We walked down Beale Street, where none of the restaurants, blues clubs, or theaters seemed in the slightest way reminiscent of downtown Minneapolis. There were no awkward meetings with former friends, no abbreviated explanations for confused acquaintances. New and sinless, I had the freedom of a stranger. Hoisting Kishke's front legs, I danced to street musicians, who overtook the riffs wafting out of the lambent and expensive pubs.

Traveling south in April seemed exceptionally fine to a person from the still-frozen North. The landscape grew greener every mile; trees started to flower and leaf as if I were watching time-lapse photography of spring. None of this splendor, though, prepared me for what happened next. Without warning, I suddenly felt my entire being drawn forward in anticipation. Kishke stood up on the seat where he had been sleeping and looked out the window. All at once out of the mist rolled blue and green mountains, layered like the limbs of enormous women lying together in a steam bath. The closer I got, the more entranced I became. Unlike the stern and craggy faces of the high Rockies, these gentle giants brimmed with every shape and size of green vegetation, the lushness punctuated with tiny flowers called bluets. This was how I met the Southern Appalachians.

The following day I hiked the Polls Gap Trail into Cataloochee Valley in the Great Smoky Mountains National Park. There, tropical-looking rhododendron sheltered roaring whitewater streams. A canopy of giant hemlock and tulip trees towered above the thick understory. Reaching open land, I again saw the soft, rolling ridges, thrown into relief by that inscrutable mist, the source of the name, Smoky Mountains.

In the western United States, fellow hikers will tell you about the miles they've covered and the elevation gain of the climb. On top of Mount Sopris in Colorado, for example, a complete stranger told me that my harrowing ascent to the top couldn't compare with Capitol Peak or his other adventures in the High Sierra. So the people I met in Cataloochee Valley surprised me very much. One told me not to miss a yellow trillium. Others described a bygone homesite and shared what they knew about the mountain people and Cherokees who once lived here. A fisherman claimed he knew every ripple of the creek because he was "practically born in it." On that particular May day, it rained without warning, as if someone took a bucket and poured it over our heads. My little dog and I were drenched, my camera ruined, and the trail became an obstacle course of water and gooey mud. Despite doubtful glances from a tired terrier, I walked the five miles out, singing like an idiot, entranced by the endless variety of green dripping around us.

During that first summer, I waited tables in Cherokee, North Carolina, on the Quallah boundary of the Eastern Band of Cherokees. Owned by a Cherokee woman, the restaurant I worked in was operated by a North Carolina family, and many Cherokees worked in the kitchen. Our customers included an interesting mix of tourists, Cherokees, and other locals. My friends in the restaurant teased me about being a Yankee, but they also filled my life with stories about the place they lived. One favorite customer, who always ordered pie and coffee no matter the time of day, told me he once saw footprints of the Little People, magical folks from old Cherokee legends, on the banks of Soco Creek.

On my days off I hiked with another new friend, a park ranger, who introduced me to the colorful names of southern mountain plants, animals, and places—doghobble, preacher birds, and Boogerman Trail. When I brought my enthusiasm for these discoveries back to the restaurant, one of my fellow waitresses joked, "I know what you are—you're one of those flower children." A late bloomer, at least, I figured.

I supplemented my tips and wages by writing articles for the *Waynesville Mountaineer* and the *Christian Science Monitor.* In addition to bear experts and hunters, elderly people and Cherokees, I interviewed a man who called himself an environmentalist, well versed in EPA regulations. Yet he didn't look like any activist I had previously encountered. He wore an old cap and a plaid shirt, and he spoke affectionately to every person who came into the store where I interviewed him. His family had lived in the mountains for generations, run moonshine during the 1920s, and he still owned this general store, much beloved by locals. His family stories frequently blended with the facts of the contemporary conflict he was describing. Members of his family had been removed from the Great Smoky Mountains so that the state could create a national park. A paper mill now rendered the nearby Pigeon River an industrial sewer. It was too late to help his ancestors, but before he died, he wanted to see the river run clear.

Although I had lived in the region only a matter of months, I recognized something new to me in the store owner and in my Cherokee friends. I appreciated the people of the Smokies because they daily manifested something I myself do not yet have: a sense of place. Historian Kirkpatrick Sale uses a Spanish word, *querencia,* to describe this state, which is more than knowing the land well or living a long time in the same acreage: It means, Sale tells us, "a home for the soul." *Querencia,* this mysterious pull on a piece of your heart from a part of the Earth, intrigued me. All the romantic characters of my youth found themselves or their purpose by setting out, pushing off, embarking on; here in the Blue Ridge, people stayed put, dug in, found home.

Everywhere I looked, there were questions to which I wanted answers. Every story told in answer seemed to beg a couple more. How did the North Carolina Cherokee escape the Trail of Tears? Why were there cemeteries in the national park? Did lumber companies just pass by the Smoky Mountains? Like a two-year-old who follows every answer with "why," I found that one question led to another, and like many with this affliction, I ended up in graduate school.

Someplace between history and people's stories, I discovered the importance of communities to a sense of place. One woman I interviewed had her eyes flood with tears when she told me about growing up in Hazel Creek. Her stories of life in the valley blended quickly with a colorful story about her marriage to a neighbor boy, who whisked her over the mountain to Tennessee, her brothers and father in hot pursuit. Another woman described drying berries on granny's rock, using pennyroyal to get rid of fleas, lying in the fields listening to church bells ring. It is nearly impossible, she seemed to say, to separate the people of Greenbrier from the land on which they lived and loved. Because both the Hazel Creek and Greenbrier communities were removed by the state governments to create the national park, their memories flashed with unexpected anger and sudden sadness.

In Cherokee I met a woman who regained her life by returning home to the mountains. A Native American raised in an all-white community in Tennessee, she suffered ridicule and embarrassment from her classmates as a child. "When you played cowboys and Indians, nobody wanted to be the Indian," she said. As an adult, her marriage and her life went downhill because of her own and her husband's alcohol abuse. She gave up drinking at a Baptist revival, then changed her life by living in the mountains and learning about her own heritage and Cherokee mythology. Many of the Cherokee myths use specific locations in the Smokies —Clingmans Dome, or *Kuwo-i,* for example, is where the Bears held a special council that turned into the creation of both disease and medicine. For my Cherokee friend, the mountains have multiple layers of meaning. More than inspiring scenery or even a well-worn mental map, the landscape shapes the character of her spiritual life.

As much as I might study mythology and history, there is something that cannot be transferred to me because I am not Cherokee and I will never live in Hazel Creek. Part of what ties a person to a piece of land is unique experiences living with it and the time to contemplate the meaning of those experiences—when the azaleas bloom, how the creek rises, why the wind can swell like a tornado, whether William Bartram crossed this valley. Like the differences between a new lover and a rich marriage, getting to know a mountain requires seeing its face in every range of light and season.

The Minnesotans who know me tell me that I replaced the love of a man with a passion for a place. "You found what you were searching for," commented my friend Ed. He was right, but not exactly in the way he intended. It would be more accurate to say that I have found the search that is mine. I want to know what my family for generations—and my culture for centuries—have tried to deny: I want to know what it means to stay.

Today I have students of my own doing oral interviews in the community. Informally, I am always collecting stories about the people who live here and the people who have created this place. I also collect heirloom seeds, which connect me to loving gardeners of the past. Yet no one in North Carolina will ever mistake me for a native. Nor can I pretend to have grandparents who built the house in which I live. But every day on the way to school, I recite the names of those around me—*Magnolia glandiflora, Liriodendron tulipfera, Opossum nuisance*—like a morning prayer. And as I reach the top of the hill that is Main Street, I am working the shape of the land to my bones.

DANCING THE CANCER
DOWN TO DUST

Julie Moulds Rybicki

JULY 2, 1994: *One week after our wedding, three months before the bone marrow transplant. My first chemotherapy, after a nine-month remission, at Midwestern Regional Medical Center (MRMC), Zion, Illinois. My fourteenth chemotherapy treatment.*

I think I'm better at surviving than living—real living, real joy. Maybe that's why I've done all right with all my months, years of chemo. It's necessary, and I'm a survivor. My husband, John, said he's the opposite. I could see him wigging out in here—the enclosed room and building you can't leave. (He's claustrophobic. Even when he has the whole world to roam around in, he still feels closed in.) The image of those evil cells eating up his body would destroy John. But John knows how to live. He is the most violently alive person I have ever known.

At living I have so often failed, caught up so often in the insignificant microdramas: grading school papers, straightening the dirty house, taking care of the mechanics of it all. I got mad at myself the other day in our honeymoon cabin. I was addressing thank you notes while John was scrawling down the beauty of our Upper Peninsula cottage on Lake Michigamme. Now, here, in a hospital room, on drugs, addressing envelopes makes sense. Trapped in a white room for five days, it's a good use for the long hazy hours.

Today I walked fifty minutes with my rolling IV around

the hospital's circular halls. The IV machine ran out of juice
and started beeping. I pushed my freedom to the limit, because normally the IV (thus me) must be connected to the
wall plug by my bed. I walked to Fred Astaire's *Shall We
Dance?* and *Swingtime* soundtracks. A glorious Radiola tape.
I felt so happy, so alive. I was in the trenches. I was a woman
of power. A newlywed. I was not going to let the evil cells
get me.

And besides, I am convinced of the curative powers of
Fred Astaire. This time around Fred will heal me. It's part
the singing. It's part Fred and Ginger's slyness. It's part the
dancing. They are *tap dancing* on the tape. You can see them,
feel them crossing a dance floor under the lights, dancing inside your body.

I think of Galway Kinnell's "Last Songs," the closest I've
ever come to having a creed: "Whatever it is that keeps us
from heaven—sloth, wrath, greed, fear—could we only re-
invent it on earth as song." And dance. For Fred and Ginger,
I must add dance.

JULY 3, 1994

I'm doing some children's literature visualizations (a way to
use the mind's power to focus on the body curing itself): I
could imagine Russia's Vasilisa the Wise pouring the Water
of Life through my veins with the chemotherapy in the IV
sacks; or Alice in Wonderland beside my bed feeding me an-
ticancer cakes; or Baba Yaga, the witch from Russian folk-
lore, eating the cancer cells like tree trunks. I'll try out
the cannibal witch. The other two are too peaceful. Wrath
makes more sense to me.

Later. I am angry at the nurse, who just said I can't be disconnected from my IV to take a shower. I ask her when can I be,

and she says, "You're on twenty-four-hour chemo," and just leaves. All the other nurses let me take a shower. She is not being helpful, and I am angry—I can't even change my shirt without being unhooked from the IV. I'm caged. And I smell because my body is sweating strange chemicals. After breakfast I will buzz her and make her help me. Be rude back.

JULY 4, 1994

The nurse on the night shift says to my roommate, Donna, "Try to sleep. Are you afraid to sleep?" Donna replies, "Yes, I'm afraid I'll die."

Jesus.

No wonder she has been fighting to keep her glazed eyes open all day.

What right do I have to feel separate from her, even superior? I've got the same demon in my body. I've had nine months' rest from cancer, gained back my lost weight and hair, look normal to the normal eye.

I see fireworks through the thick window in my hospital room. Gold, spermy light. Will I have children? Should I worry about fertility when my general survival is at stake? The woman in the next bed—skull, bones, and slack skin— is being *eaten alive*, is afraid to sleep. Afraid she'll die in it.

One flaming rocket just up, round and bright as my last week's bridal bouquet. I can see the Fourth of July onlookers, listen to their catcalls dimly through the glass. They feel like ghost people, muffled, separate from me. Donna and I are like bruises beneath the hospital's skin.

More explosions. A heart. A sky sparkler. A garden. A carnation. I am alive in this world. Purple is my color. I share a room with someone who is too tired to eat, fighting for her life. A green burst for life. White for hope. Pink for love. Gold for magic. I can barely hear them out there with their watered-down crowd sounds, their oohing and aahing. A red for passion. A peacock. A sequined '20s dress. The hospital room is reflecting off the dark glass: white curtains, blinking red lights, the white curtain separating me from death. Outside, an explosion of colored flowers and stars. "She's in a position where she can't see the fireworks," the nurse says. "How sad."

The fireworks end suddenly. Lightning strikes, so the City of Zion stops the show. It's my second round of chemotherapy treatments. (I've already had thirteen months'.) It is the second round, first chemo, fourth day, Fourth of July. Not the first holiday I've spent in here.

No Benadryl this chemo until tonight. That's why I've been so clearheaded, which isn't my usual here. I don't need all the Benadryl they pump into me. I'm going to tell them not to use it on me anymore, or at least to cut the dose in half. It makes me too dopey, and I have a say.

I am Dorothy, blue ginghamed and virginal—able to face down mock wizards and lions.

Just before I sleep, my John telephones, says to me, "I'm surprised the hospital hasn't grown chicken legs, like Baba Yaga's house, and swum across Lake Michigan to bring you back to me."

JULY 5, 1994: *A later memory of July 4*

The nurse said to my roommate, "Donna, try to sleep. Why won't you sleep?"

Donna replied, "Because I might die." She knew how close she was. She was tenacious of life. Though later that night she repeatedly took off her respirator in our black room. I wondered if delirium or desperation was her motive. I lay in the darkness, in my hospital bed, listening for the change in her breathing when the respirator was off. (The rhythmic hissing would stop.) Then I buzzed the nurse alert. After several episodes, the nurse connected the respirator to her face with strong tape so Donna could no longer remove it.

Why did I keep buzzing the nurses? She was suffering so much, death would have been a relief to her. I guess I did not want Donna to die while I was in the room.

JULY 19, 1994: *From our home in Richland, Michigan*

Today I saw giant turtles mating at the zoo. My friend Ruth, her son Brendan, and I first heard the sound: a long oomph, a pause; a loud ooomph, a pause. He took his time, slowly enjoying his business. And in front of the children no less. The zoo creatures all had mates, except for one or two, someone to sing or squawk or bleat or chatter or moo with. I also received a letter saying my bone marrow transplant had been deemed appropriate by my insurance company. Thank God. The go-ahead has been granted. I phone-interviewed with Social Security, $500 a month when I'm sick, which will help because my bills aren't going away. The doctors say I shouldn't work for at least six months. Things were already tight on my university part-timer income. Part-time instructors make a pittance.

Later, we—John, Ruth, her four-year-old Brendan, and I—had a blanket picnic in our yard, had a distilled water fight and jumped rope, playing snake and chase the end of the line. It was glorious.

And my hair is falling out like crazy. I pick at it like a scab, pulling it out in fingerfuls, ironing my scarves. I take a gold, blue, red, and green one, tie it to a straw hat. Tomorrow I will go to the barbershop and have what's left of my hair chopped off, butched. It's hard to see it go piece by piece. On the news tonight, a woman with breast cancer had just found out, after a remission, that her cancer had come back; it metastasized to her brain, lung, liver. She talked about really living, how each day is a gift.

Living is better than language.

JULY 20, 1994: *Richland, Michigan*

This morning I stood in the shower, water pounding on my head, until the last 70 percent of my hair fell out. I was there a long time. I'd scoop a big handful of hair off the drain. More would fall. I'd kneel down in the pulsing water and keep scooping handful after handful onto the yellow bathroom mat to keep the drain clear. I've saved all my hair from the last few days, set it in a pile on my dresser. I don't know why. I just wanted it. It had come back so beautiful: darker, almost black, with no gray, and curlier than it has been since I was six. I went in the shower with diminished yet respectable hair and came out almost bald. Only a few odd hunks survived—I looked comical, grotesque. All the cue-ball people came to mind (some by shaver): Yul Brynner, Sinead O'Connor, Captain Picard, Uncle Fester.

Bald. Bald. Bald. In a way I'm excited about my cue-ball head. About the gaudy ways I will adorn it: bright African hats, silk scarves, red bandannas, and purple baseball caps from bars. I have a large selection assembled from my first time through this.

Another new experience: going to the barber. I decided to go all the way. The 5 percent of surviving hair—ugly clumps on the top of my head and a Mohawk strip down the back—had to go. If I'm going to be bald, I'll be bald. No pitiful clumps and sad wisps. I'm going for the Woman of Power look.

It was odd stepping into the lime-green-walled, male domain of the barbershop. It was right after lunch, 1 P.M., and he unlocked the door to let me in. "I've never had my hair cut at a barbershop before," I said.

"It's not like going to the moon," he said, and proceeded to shave off my tufts.

It was too damn quiet in that room and in that chair, so I told the barber how the second batch of hair had been so much nicer than the first.

"That's because it was healthier hair," he said in the tone of one who really knows. Anyway, there wasn't much to work with, but he took his time, clipping it and shaving it again, using a little vacuum cleaner to suck the stubble off my head and neck, brushing off my now-pink skull. He charged me full price.

I came home and John was typing. I yelled, "I'm bald! I'm bald!" and whipped off my hat and headband and spread my arms and started spinning in a circle. I started to dance because this has to be funny. I have to make this funny.

AUGUST 28, 1994: *Richland, Michigan*

When you are in danger, the adrenaline quickens, your senses are heightened. You realize, *I am not dead.* I could be soon, but I am not now. And each day means more than it ever has. You are on the edge of a canyon fighting the winds. The cancer has tried to get me, but you see, it hasn't gotten me yet. I might be different if it was eating me alive, which it would like to do. I have seen some husks of people it has done that to. I am singing and building walls against it: Not me Not me Not me.

John said he'd shave his head bald, like those ten-year-old boys did in a chemo-boy's class. Shaved their heads in support. I told him he had great hair. Sometimes when I am lonely and have to get it out, I'll tell him, "Your hair looks tense." He'll laugh his way down into my arms, and I'll stroke his hair and hold him close. I ask how can he love someone with a bowling-ball head. He says he loves me more, that I went bald just so he would love me more. He is holding me and kissing my stub head and telling me he can see all the hair holes in my skull. Then he starts sucking out all my brains with loud slurping sounds. He says the big pile of my hair on the dresser is grossing him out and would I please put it away.

SEPTEMBER 7, 1994: *Richland, Michigan*

Fevers in the middle of the night, mouth sores, five to seven interferon shots a month, men and women walking around the hospital with their rolling IVs in tow. I know the routine by now, and I keep telling everyone Fred Astaire is going to cure me and remembering my wedding two and a half months ago when I danced barefoot across the grass with John in my arms. There is this Christian singer, Julie Miller, I really like—she got me through my first thirteen months of chemo. I could hear the pain in her voice. If I've seemed happy lately, it is not because I am minimizing the pain of cancer: Six treatments into my first round of chemotherapy, I was down to ninety-some pounds, barely able to eat for weeks due to loss of appetite and mouth sores. I've gone home so my mother would force feed me, once an hour, until some of my strength came back. I've coughed so hard, I've had to let my college classes out early. I've sat absolutely still on my sofa at home because that stillness seemed to be the only thing to quell my nausea. In some ways I've had a lonely, miserable, inward life, and I understand misery.

I thank God for John. He says I have this well of loneliness in me he can't quite loop his arms around. He has let me pour all those years of love into him. He has returned me to light and love.

OCTOBER 15, 1994: *An ice cream shop in Portage, Michigan. The day before we travel to the cancer hospital.*

John just stuck the ice cream cone to his forehead. The jack-o'-lantern in the ice cream shop window looks ominous with its black orifices, its rotting head. John says something to me in Spanish that I don't understand. I do not ask what he means. It's cold in here, I say, sucking down my tea. I am thirty-one. In this glorious, portentous evening, before the jaws close around me, I am thinking—*Jesus, I still have to go to the Laundromat tonight.* That's why John is the poet of the family. When John is transcendent, heavenly, I am in the Laundromat, or counting how many shots the doctors can give me in one day.

Since we are two doors away, we go to the big bookstore, John Rollins. I buy a book of thirty Civil War postcards from the sale table. I will send them to my friends when I am in the bone marrow unit, signed, "news from the front." Whether or not others think so, at this moment, that seems funny. I am writing in the dark car, John driving. I have a hacking cough, and my body is trying to choke. John is singing "The Girl from Ipanema." John has been giving me shots to put my bone marrow production into overdrive. I feel the marrow growing in my hips. It pulses strangely.

EDITORS' NOTE: *From October 20 to October 23, Julie received high-dose chemotherapy, five to seven times the normal amount of treatment, and enough to kill a person in a normal situation. She was heavily medicated, and her journal entries are lines like: "I've been asleep for eighteen hours."*

OCTOBER 27, 1994: *MRMC, 6:50 A.M., five days after high-dose chemotherapy ended. Day eleven in the unit.*

I've gained seven pounds in the bone marrow unit, most of it water weight—I'm being pumped with fluids twenty-four hours a day. I want to scratch, claw, the dark rash that has covered my body from my neck down. I show remarkable restraint. My head has been hurting since last night. The nurse, Hyun Choi, gets me an ice pack to cool it.

My white blood cells have dropped to 0.2 (200 out of a normal 5,000 to 10,000). I wear my mask because the cleaning lady is here. She works nearly forty minutes a day on each room in this unit, wiping down and disinfecting everything. Also, the furniture is nonporous, and the ceilings have special air filters in them to keep down the dust and fungi.

2 P.M. ILLness time. (My stupid joke. This is ILLinois.) It feels good to be free of my IV right now. (I took a shower and they have to disconnect you for that.) Unfortunately, I am not free from my Foley catheter. But it feels good to be clean and to not smell like chemicals. I've been unattached an hour now but have decided to let the nurses forget about me for a bit longer. I will enjoy my mobility in this ten-by-twenty-foot room that I can't leave.

I turned on my very first soap opera of this incarceration, *General Hospital*, a show I've watched either casually or with addiction for twenty years now. I know the character Monica has breast cancer on the show now; I wonder how they deal with it on TV.

They transfused me earlier with albumin, a blood product, and I will have another transfusion today. My own blood is nearly dead. Because I don't really want to think about it, I may seem careless about this bone marrow transplant process. (Denial can be a great survival mechanism.) But if I were in the regular world, without air filters, blood transfusions, antibiotics, and antifungals—I'd be dead. Pure and simple. If 5,000 white blood cells is low normal, I have, at this moment, a mere 4 percent of an immune system.

OCTOBER 28, 1994: *MRMC. Day 12 in the bone marrow unit.*

I exercised on the stationary bike today! It's possible even with a rolling IV if you move the bike near the electrical outlet, with your IV machine plugged into the wall. Later John told me he imagined the bike breaking free and me crashing through my room's glass windows, me flying over the city park. But I would never have thought of that. John would write with more passion if he were in here. I will do my best, documenting tests and dinners and the ways I evade thinking about repercussions—the repercussions of the success or failure of my mission here. But I fear people who read about this will want more than my sterile accounts.

I fell asleep listening to a mystery book on tape (one of my hospital entertainments). I woke up, then turned off the running cassette recorder. Reading this bone marrow transplant newsletter is very discouraging. The section on low-grade non-Hodgkins lymphoma talks about how sneaky this strain of lymphoma can be, about its frequent recurrences.

It is late evening. I sound selfish, but John only called twice today, before and after work, and I am heartbroken. (I also talked tonight with my parents and my good friend, Jenny LaHaie.) John, please call tonight, before I go to sleep, the most important call of the day.

I love John so much. If I could, I would be enveloping him with love in the kitchen, where he is most likely typing right now.

OCTOBER 29, 1994: *MRMC. Day 13 in the unit.*

Everything tastes and smells differently when you're having chemotherapy. The thought, the smell of coffee, which I normally worship, makes me sick in here. Plain tea is best. In general, plain everything is best. I've stopped ordering regular hospital concoctions, and I generally eat unadorned Cream of Wheat or yogurt or mashed potatoes, broth soups or half sandwiches. Sometimes canned fruits or vegetables. All my favorites must be canned—they contain fewer germs than fresh.

NOVEMBER 1, 1994: *MRMC. Day 14 in the unit, 6:45 A.M.*

It looks like 8 A.M., it's so bright. I'm studying the movement of the sun in here. Tracy, the other woman in the bone marrow unit, died last night. Her parents and husband were there, and her brothers had flown to see her this weekend. We weren't friends, but we were friendly. She was the same age as me, give or take a year. I liked her; she had an attitude, a sharp sense of humor, an edge. She is my shadow because she was my age, and I liked her. But I cannot let myself compare myself with her.

This is the seventh day I can't leave the room; the beginning of my third week at the hospital. Tracy just died. She had been fighting her Hodgkin's disease for over ten years, her longest remission only lasting nine months. Her fight has been pretty constant: Hodgkin's, chemo, blood tests, hospitals.

I spent one year in heavy-duty chemotherapy, thirteen five-day, in-hospital treatments. At home, John gave me interferon shots (a drug that was supposed to build up my immune system) two nights a week. After each shot, at about four in the morning, I would wake up, freezing, though actually hot with fevers. The fevers gave me mouth sores; the mouth sores made it so painful to eat, I eventually dropped to under one hundred pounds and could only eat with gums numbed by medications, my meals consisting of frozen yogurt or high-calorie vitamin shakes. I was tired from the chemo, tired from teaching over thirty hours a week at the university to keep my insurance. I spent a lot of time preparing for my classes so I would not lose my job benefits. (They recently got cut anyway. God bless the COBRA program. God damn universities that treat their part-time instructors like less-than-human beings. The administrators who cut my benefits knew I had cancer.) I was too weak to carry my books to class, so my parents bought me a rolling bag-lady cart for Christmas. Other professors helped me cover the one or two class days a month when I was out of state having chemotherapy treatments.

It was a very bad year, August 1992 to August 1993. I slept a lot. I would sit in one spot on the couch, very still, to lessen my nausea. Can I imagine the year I spent in heavy-duty multiplied by ten? All those shots and mouth sores. All that weight and strength and breath loss. All that time in survival mode. After that first year, I got a nine-month break and an easy three-month chemo tour. I was all fattened up from my wedding (which was very curative), all rested because I wasn't working. Also, the second time around, there was no interferon, so there were no shots and no fevers. Yes, a much easier run.

I think of Tracy. She had to have her lungs drained a week back, that I know of. (I stopped by her room twelve days ago, before I was put in isolation.) She was in such pain that it hurt her to talk. Her marriage was struggling, and that was getting her down.

Bless Tracy's spirit. May it be in a good place without the suffering of her last decade.

Bless Tracy's family. Her mom (whom she talked with a lot), her dad, brothers, and the rest.

Bless Tracy's husband. Help him with his grief. Let God, not humanity, judge whether his leaving her pushed her to her death. It wouldn't be the first time illness ended a marriage. Don't let it happen to my John and me.

Bless me. And let me live a long and happy life with John. Let my cancer be cured. Let us have a baby, even. Bless me with the continued support of John, my parents, my family, my friends. Bless our writing.

Bless Tracy one more time. We only met four or five times, but I liked her. She is, was sharp-edged, funny, and determined. Take her to the place where there is no pain.

Amen.

NOVEMBER 2, 1994: *MRMC. Day 15 in the unit.*

My white blood count has leaped to 0.5! (That's 500 out of a normal 5,000 to 10,000 white blood cells.) May it keep improving. Every leap in counts means my immune system is starting to regenerate. I feel tired today. This is my schedule so far:

5 A.M.: Blood draw; I have a sore throat, so I gargled and got some Tylenol from the nurse.

8 A.M.: I ate breakfast: Cream of Wheat, cold tea, a half pint skim milk.

8:15 A.M.: Patty, the head nurse/administrator of the bone marrow unit, and another woman check out my mouth, which is deteriorating due to the high-dose chemo.

8:30 A.M.: I have an EKG. They want a bowel movement sample, and I get in trouble for putting the stool in the lab container myself.

8:35 A.M.: Barbara, my nurse, checks out my mouth and says to gargle fifteen times a day with saline to help heal it.

9:00 A.M.: I have an X-ray done. (They wheel in a portable machine.)

9:05 A.M.: I put antibacterial cream up my dry nostrils to keep them from bleeding.

9:10 A.M.: I fill out my paperwork (my input and output sheet tracking my food, drink, urine, vomit, and bowel movements) and fill out my menu for tomorrow.

The life of a busy BMT executive. And all of it without leaving my room, too.

NOVEMBER 12, 1994: *MRMC. Day 25 in the unit.*

I need to get writing because my parents (who have come up every weekend, bless them, and played a dozen games of Rummy 500 to pass our time) will be here any minute. Now that I know I will leave here soon, now that the actual procedure is over, I worry.

What next? The Big Bone Marrow Transplant is, was my great hope for cure, my salvation, my chance. But what if it failed? What if, on my first CAT scans and evaluation, some cancer shows up? What if my big gun is shot, and it misfired? What will they do? Drag out my chemotherapy until the cancer spreads somewhere they can't treat it? (For lymphomas, there is less and less chance for a permanent cure as the chemotherapy goes on. Chemo might lengthen life but will most likely not cure the patient of disease.) Eventually I'd be locked down in a failing body like Tracy was.

I am happy now because I have a great love and I have hope. Hope for a cure. Hope for a long life. I even have hopes for children. But in the back of my head, I keep hearing *what if, what if, what if.* What if I should have waited until the little tumor in my abdomen (where my cancer recurred) had totally disappeared before I started the BMT process; started with a clean slate. I have had the BMT, and there's no other real, hopeful option for a cure for me, except perhaps a second one. What if, what if, what if. What if this doesn't work.

What I have had all along is the belief that I would beat this thing. The belief that it wouldn't get me. The love of John, whom I need and who needs me. I want to live with him until we are old. Be old greyhounds together on the porch of our slightly ratty home, still talking of our courtship in graduate school. How he thought I was the prettiest woman he'd seen in years. The way he showed me how to partner dance, as he had shown "his" kids from the Detroit Children's Home, for their talent show at camp. I was in his office, the door open, only about a half hour after we'd really met. I wasn't sure exactly what to think, except that I liked his enthusiasm for the world. I, we, would remember what happened the first time I told him I loved him. It was near Christmas (three and a half months after we met). We were cleaning up after a holiday party at my apartment, everyone else had left, and the words just slipped out of me. I was shocked and surprised because I wasn't conscious I loved him until I actually said the words. I started to cry and he held me.

It would be a miracle to be cured and to be able to bear

our children. I know, even if I am cured, I may be sterile from the procedures I've been through, but I guess now isn't the time to think about that. My life is what's most important now. So much is riding on this BMT.

EDITORS' NOTE: Julie Moulds Rybicki's disease was in remission for three years. In 1998 she began treatment again.

CHANGING TERRAIN

DIANE GLANCY

I stopped at my former mother-in-law's house in St. Joseph, Missouri, on my way from Minnesota to Texas. My son had just moved into a place near Midlothian, south of Dallas. On the way I picked up some of the things he left at his grandmother's during his moving-around years. A handyman helped me load the car. *You're the first wife,* he said. Afterward, driving to Kansas City where I would stay with my daughter before I drove on to Texas, I thought of the years as the *first wife* when I had traveled to my mother-in-law's house with my children and husband. Now those years were over. I had been married nineteen years. I have been divorced fifteen. There was a vague feeling of accomplishment at being on my own, but I also felt *alone* as I drove back to the interstate. Then too, there was the *leftover* sadness I felt from those early years. Marriage had not been satisfying. I also was sorry it had not worked out.

There are some constants: the Missouri limestone outcroppings along the interstate. The flint hills in Kansas, the only part of I-35 where there is a tollgate. I can drive from St. Paul through Texas, and the only place I pay a toll is in Kansas. That's the part of the road I'd call *marriage.* But I like to drive through the rolling short-grass hills on the top shelf of the prairie, just under the sky. I also notice the gray-green flint along the road where the grass wears thin.

Once through Kansas, in Oklahoma, I watch for the Cimarron River, the Washita River, the red ponds red from the red soil. Also the Arbuckle Anticline. The Red River into Texas.

It is a change I am grateful for. The later years. On my own. Responsible for my own living. Making my own income. Independent. Because I have to be.

I remember the years as artist-in-residence for the Arts Council of Oklahoma. Traveling from school to school, staying in places that were not mine. Feeling disconnected from self, from place. I remember pounding the nothingness with my words as I wrote, knowing someday they'd go somewhere.

Now I have a house and a job, even if they're in Minnesota. I have the change from the insecurity of an unhappy marriage and an unsteady husband. I have tenure. There is some security in that. I have dated the same man for nearly seven years. We probably will leave it at that.

My daughter also had sent some boxes for my son, heavy boxes of dishes and cookware. I had a large box of tools in the back of the car, his weights, a ladder, and several boxes of books I was taking to a conference in Texas I also would attend over the semester break. Why else would I drive a thousand miles in early January with my station wagon dragging in back?

Unpacking the dishes my daughter handed down to my son also took me back to when my marriage and housekeeping were new. I was still unpacking, but in a different way, on another level. I was unpacking for someone else who was just starting out. I saw all the work that needed done on the house. I was glad to be beyond that.

I think of the word *transition*. There are contradictions in it. Over the years, I ran. I also sat. Both are included in the act of transition. I still feel outside my life. The years have brought changes for the better, but there's a vitality, an expectation of the future I see in my grown children that I don't feel. Yet I'm glad I'm where I am.

I have a place mainly through writing—what I do with

my hands on the letters of the alphabet. It's not an overt fist fight, but a *wrist fight*. A quiet fight of thought and planning and determination and not giving up. But that has been with me for a while. The change is that I have a chance to use it.

I return to my son's house after the writers' conference in Belton, which is nearly two hours south of Midlothian on I-35. Then I have a reading at the Sequoyah Bookstore in Dallas, and afterward I want to start home.

An anticline is a place of stratified rock that slopes down on each side from its crest. In other words, some old upheaval pushed part of the bedrock to the surface. The Arbuckle Anticline is what I-35 climbs toward in Oklahoma, before dropping into Texas. It's what I climb again, heading north on my return from Texas, back into Oklahoma. I will pass through Kansas and the tollgate again. Then Missouri, Iowa, and Minnesota, where it is twelve below.

My son and my daughter and I live close to I-35. The same interstate connects us, though we live many hundreds of miles apart.

I stay with my daughter in Kansas City for another night. The next day I drive on, smelling of dog and a spot of spilled coffee on my coat and a trace of gasoline on my glove. The early morning is icy. On the road to downtown Kansas City, where I connect with the interstate, I fight with words to establish my identity and place. I fight with words to speak my survival into existence. Then I drive seven hours back to Minnesota in the cold. The *first wife* carrying a car loaded with a leftover sadness. My former husband and I had not connected in marriage. I couldn't live with the emptiness but entered a greater emptiness of the world when I divorced, where I would make my way. I have a sense of failure because my marriage did not work out, yet at the same time, I have a sense of relief as I drive the changing terrain of my life.

CROSSING OVER

KATHLEEN CARR

I tease that it all began with a picnic during which I fell and cut my forehead:

It was the strangest summer. One evening, ripe with wine and laughter and searching for a waterfall, I fell upon a stone. Twenty-one stitches along the hairline. Paula, my friend, you came to visit. You fed me soup of green and yellow squash. How carefully you snipped the garlic chives and placed the borage blossoms in our bowls and never gave yourself away. You sat beside me in the perfumed dusk. I had to fight for breath.

Two weeks later Paula sent me the following note:

I'm an awful coward about the simplest/most complex things like talking about personal feelings. I have therefore decided to use this strange method halfway between writing and speaking* to tell you that I love you, and if this were to include x-rated activity, I'd be most happy. If not, if in fact dreams are necessarily separate from reality, I love you anyway and hope that you aren't annoyed or offended at my having been presumptuous, etc. I foolishly bumble through

* On the front of the folded sheet of paper were these words: "A note to be read in my presence so that we can talk along with it if you want."

life falling in love with people—can't help it. Maybe this paper should be chewed up and swallowed along with a piece
of string.

(During the next three weeks, Paula and I met and wrote
often, trying to intellectualize/rationalize, understand this
thing that was happening to us.)

LETTER # 1: *July 23, 1994*
Dear Paula,
    Well, I know why the butterflies congregate and hover
above my flower garden, P; with *us,* after three weeks of our
having lived daily with internal butterflies, they feel wonderfully at home. Good morning. I saw you only twelve
hours ago, but I need to say some things. Funny, each time
we talk, I feel resolved about so many things, but once you
leave, thoughts and questions race through my mind. (Is
that where thoughts/questions form, do you think? Or in
one's body, as well?) I had a restless (wonderful-restless) evening and an extremely restless (not wonderful-restless but
not bad either) night. I didn't want you to leave; I felt that we
could have talked all night (notice I said *talked*).
    One of the things that I tried to articulate last night
(some of my words seemed to cause you pain, Paula; you
said no but you looked yes) revolved around a question I
asked aloud but was really asking of myself: How could I
even *know* if I were in love with and/or sexually attracted to
a woman (you)? The correct and sensible thing is to say it
doesn't make any difference, a person's sex. Ideally, yes.
    But what about someone who has actually believed
(Why? I'm not sure; as part of her social construct, perhaps?)
that she is completely heterosexual? *If* (aren't italics wonderful?) she believed this (for whatever foolish reasons) (aren't
parentheses wonderful?) but there's a possibility that it isn't

so, she would experience such a rupture—a tear in her
being* that she would be "other" than what she *is*—and perhaps that has been too frightening for her to acknowledge
consciously. So any feelings she might have for a woman
similar to those she has had for men (and if she is honest, she
must admit those feelings have surfaced before; at the time,
she rolled them quizzically around in her mind [and body],
asking herself: What if, someday, I were to *become* lesbian?
But the thoughts remained safely inside—*she* remained
safely inside), she would rationalize or intellectualize them
away. She has always been good at that.

What I'd most like you to understand, Paula, is that this
isn't *about* sexuality (or shouldn't be; *I* am the one acting as
though it is)—it's about *being*—*my* being. It has taken me
fifty years of hard work, alone, to develop a strong, independent, capable, healthy (relatively) sense of myself (selves),
and part of that self is (was) a heterosexual. If I am not that,
then I am not I.

> Kathleen = heterosexual female
> heterosexual female dies
> therefore, Kathleen dies

(I know, I know, I hear you: She can be reborn.) You have
challenged not only (the narrowness of) my entire world
but the/my concept of who I am. You have challenged me
to be, have told me that I *can* be, have said that you will *show
me how* to be other than I am—"Other."

LETTER # 2: *July 24*
Paula, you are one of the most courageous and beautiful

---

* I see now that I *have* been attaching my sexuality to a "constructed" (social,
cultural, psychological?) self, instead of to my *being*, where it belongs . . . female.
If I am not that (Foucault is right: Why do we have to be an *any*-sexual being?
Why not simply [a] being? You *can* be: I have yet to learn that), then I am not I.

women I know—not to mention brilliant!—and feelings for you that I didn't know I had (or didn't *allow* myself to have) have begun to surface. You have always intrigued me, woman; from the beginning there has been a tension that I couldn't identify, an attraction, something both exhilarating and frightening (my favorite word lately). I'm remembering those evenings three summers ago when we first met: We went to the Boat House for drinks; I backed off to keep myself "safe." It had always worked before.

The excitement, the possibility of loving/being loved by someone who "knows" the *jouisspace** and would participate within it with honesty and integrity, is an almost overwhelming thought/feeling and makes my stomach hurt—those damned mourning cloaks again!†

O I wish that I could give you right now Molly Bloom's answer ("and yes I said yes I will Yes"),‡ but the truth is that I am *still* confused, though less so (I don't know who I am); *still* frightened, though less so (I'm not sure I know *how* to love, except from a [safe?] distance)—both issues that I need to take up with new vigor when I return from the UK. [I had received a scholarship to study poetry for three weeks in Northern Ireland.]

I'm sorry, Paula, that I can't approach all this more lightfully, playfully, but I'm afraid my chakras are out of line/light; I'm forgetting the words of the *Tao*—hell! not only have I forgotten them, I can't find the goddamned book. Anyway, since I have much further to go in terms of alignment than you do, at least in this area, I don't expect you to wait around to see what happens—you could *die* waiting—and life's so short. . . .

---

* A word that I coined, a combination of *l'espace* and Julia Kristeva's *jouissance*, referring to the space in which art and love occur.

† A butterfly of the tortoise-shell species.

‡ James Joyce, *Ulysses.*

LETTER # 3: *Monday, August 1*
Today I leave for Islandmagee. I've been awake since 5:30
A.M., my body filled with such longing:

IN THE GARDEN

After you've gone
    your words' curves hum in the hollow
rain above the path:
    beginning
        /joy (radiant!)
gentle I would
    /will be:
I feel myself begin to open
against my will, sloe's duskblush,
the woman beneath the woman.
      Here in this garden
's ripening curve,
I wait for you
to come again.

Paula, this poem began to come to me in the middle of
the night, after we had been at Decker's, the place of things
hidden: I was excited to have written it; it felt completely
rooted in sexual passion—for *me* a miracle to have a poem
arise from that place. (I love that the Chinese characters for
"arise" are literally "rise/come.") But I was afraid to give it
to you, perhaps because it makes me feel vulnerable in a way
that I rarely acknowledge to another.

In your 7/26 letter, the words "I ache to touch you"
leapt from the page like one of Bashō's frogs. (I talked with
you less than an hour ago; it is hard for me to think to write,
to hold the pen.) On Friday (into Saturday) as we sat by the
pool, *I* ached to touch *you*, lightly, a "beginning touch," on
your arm, or to hold your hand. But my usual self, I felt shy
and frightened. Last night, when we said good-bye? I
haven't processed that yet. I don't want to. I want to let the

feelings just come when they will, "wash over me," I think you said. I *do* remember the sound of your breathing beside the cicadas' song, the brushstroke of your lips against my cheek, my mouth, my face. . . .

. . . .

(Cut on dotted line; keep top portion.)

This is the "careful, thoughtful, honest" (your words) Kathleen speaking: P.S. I don't know when, or how often, I'll write to you from Northern Ireland. Part of me wants terribly to have these three weeks to not-think, to leave my entire life behind (although I hadn't planned on your being/ becoming such a part of it), to "see" how I "feel" with some distance—from everything, everyone. I believe this will be a significant journey for me; perhaps this time, it will be *out of* instead of *into* the heart of darkness.

Part of me doesn't want to leave at all, Paula. We feel too new. Do you think it is possible for two people to sustain that feeling? To *always* feel new? (How would you sketch "us" now? Paint us?) So, if you don't hear from me for a while, it's because I'm trying to clear my head (although I'm beginning to love its whirling, spinning, dizzying), get some perspective (your thinking's rubbing off . . . perspective on what? why? something formless, encompassing *all* perspective . . . *none*). Talk about approach/avoidance. Dance. I'm a master, aren't I? You are incorrigible, relentless, and beautiful as your words.

LEAVING HOME

    black and black is the Irish Sea
    Larne appears, barely
    (so smooth so pure
    so straight her dives
    into the
            water)

gray sky
blue Ireland
water black as stone
wake white
foam
            dispersed

how many women are drawn
to the prow of a ship
because they are lonely
to the edge of a garden
how many
            women

LETTER # 4: *A running letter, beginning on August 3 in Southall, England*
Good morning, person to whom I said I might not be writing for some time; finished Baudrillard's *The Ecstasy of Communication*. A sentence that speaks to your caution re therapy: "Divested of his fantasies, he becomes eminently vulnerable to psychology"; I think, Paula, that exactly the opposite will happen for me; psychology will help me to *recover* those fantasies! Remember that I've experienced/am experiencing an irruption, a brisance that neither of us could have imagined. (As you said, a simple *yes* or *no* would have sufficed.) I'm finally looking at some things that I've been *deliberately* (on some level) *not* examining. But I'm also beginning to feel too alive to retreat, to not examine, to not love *with my body*. You have been an amazing catalyst for me, Paula. A session or two of therapy with someone I can trust is essential (remember that I've *done* counseling for eight years). *All* of me is teeming; I can sometimes—literally— barely breathe.

And I'm concerned that you may not have anyone to talk to about what is happening. I know you don't talk easily about feelings, but this seems a time for a good friend: to listen, to give a reality (or unreality) check. Do you have such a one?

As I reread the above, I think of the incredible *depth* of feeling in your letters, poems; recalling them transfuses me with warmth—no, with burning! I wanted distance from you (to some extent, I have it), but I brought your letters with me. I read them every night. I read them last night. I had a good sleep. What is that, you ask? Dreams? No dreams; I didn't need any.

LETTER # 5: *August 8, Islandmagee, Northern Ireland*
Paula,

I tried not to read your letter when I found it on my bed this evening: "Out of sight, out of mind." But I wanted to. I did. I love your "drawing" of us (will you do it?) as I love your description of the moon shining after the storm: "was it first light . . . a tear in the darkness?" Tell me you aren't deliberately seducing me with words. . . .

When I asked you if you were afraid, you said you feared that if we loved each other sexually, it might not be as good as you had imagined/hoped. (Fantasies are necessary but sometimes dangerous things, aren't they?) I have two fears to your one. In addition to the original—of loving, *period!*—I now have a fear that's similar to yours: How could we *ever* connect with our bodies to the extent that we do with our minds; how could we *ever* love to the extent that our words love on paper (particularly yours)? It *still* doesn't seem possible to me, *still* scares the shit out of me: How would I learn to do that? Have you ever loved that completely before? The thought of it weakens me.

Re: anxiety (yours): Paula (I like your name; it is like a brushstroke), there isn't anything that you could say to me, I don't think, that would feel wrong. But I *am* afraid (there's that word again) to ask you to become more physically bold—it might (two-syllable word) me away. I'm amazed that I haven't (two-syllable word) you away. Why haven't I?

Yes, I want to listen to Glenn Gould playing Bach's *Goldberg Variations*. After I come home. (*Is* it home anymore? Where *is* home?) And yes, it is excruciatingly beautiful. I love the word *excruciating* attached to *beauty:* It speaks to the incredible melancholy, sadness that music somehow encompasses, calls forth—excruciatingly beautiful—as are your letters for me; as love should be. As you are. And no, I'm not teasing you, playing with your feelings, Paula; I'm trying to find my way, perhaps *our* way.

I have a therapy appointment on Thursday, August 22. I'd like to try to stabilize things at home (although it may no longer be possible). What I'm trying to say, Paula, is that it may take some time after I return home to call you, longer to see you. Christ! I have you sounding like a mistress without the *good* stuff! Convention sucks. But then you already know that. And I'm not liking myself a whole lot for saying *any* of this; you deserve better. You're asking for something that should be simple. But it already isn't, is it? Was it ever? Could it ever be? Somehow, I doubt it. . . .

There was a large school of dolphins today near the beach. Wouldn't it be wonderful (discovery) to lie on the sand at night (joining) listening to the Irish sea (unleashing) pushing, pulsing, sometimes gently (restraint), sometimes relentlessly (assertion) against the rocky shore; lighthouse beams occasionally, rhythmically interrupting the darkness . . . such a large darkness; such rare and miraculous illuminations.

Tonight as I walked home from the Poets' House, there were still pinks and blues in the west, enough light to see by. The wind *literally* whistled across the harbor, over the farm. The grasses bent. And shall I tell you that each night when I return to my room, it is you, and only you, I think about? I imagine that you are lying beside me: One of the things I love most about you, Paula, is that each time we look at a surface, there are already so many depths that we have explored beneath it together (and somehow we know that, wordlessly); I wonder how many more there are to be seen, felt. I don't know what will become of us, but I thank you for loving me in a way *already* more wonderful than I have ever been loved before. And now I lay me down to sleep, perchance to dream ... dreams and reality—*are* they different, she asks? The same? Lights out; beacons (and moon); a ship's lights, extending in a row, extending space; outside my window; in. . . .

<blockquote>

        gasping for breath
              o
             your breath
     on my shoulder
         blade
            burning me
      inwardly spiraling we
           light
     on the borage:
     your hand near its blossom
     easing me from my stem

</blockquote>

LETTER # 6: *7:05 A.M., Saturday, August 27, back from Ireland*
Dear P,

Seduction with peaches! Both taste and presentation were delicious. Thank you for a wonderful afternoon: good food, good wine, good conversation, good feelings. I know now why I hadn't wanted to see you right away; at dinner last night [at home], I had a hard time concentrating. I kept seeing you, your smile; kept thinking how good (that word again: I must elevate my vocabulary) it was to be with you, how pretty you looked, etc., etc.

LETTER # 7: *Sunday morning, August 28*
I've been awake since 5:30, my body filled with such longing (there's hope for you yet) that I couldn't sleep. Of course, it

didn't help that I read from *The Songs of Bilitis* before going to bed. A line from your letter keeps echoing in my head: "Help me. Touch me." I want to say *soon,* Paula; I think it can be soon.

"Loves without motives last the longest." I like these words from Louy's introduction to *The Songs.* And perhaps we could substitute the word *expectations.* I'm rereading your letter re our language entanglement (pun intended) re sexual expectations. When I'm with you, I don't have *any* expectations. I like how I feel at the moment. And what I meant had nothing to do with technique. I think technique manifests itself *as* two people love, love more deeply—that it is secondary to the love, the passion. Am I being naive? It is so hard to articulate complex feelings, isn't it? But wonderful fun trying. I'll try again:

I have loved you intellectually for a long time; I'm beginning to know you emotionally and to love that part of you as well. I love your sensuousness, your sensuality—art, food, gardening, nature, language: Things I too have always loved have a hidden dimension in your presence.

Intellect, feelings, sexual desire—I have never loved someone on all three levels before (although I long for that; sex without the other two lacks a certain integrity). Nor has anyone loved me on all those levels. The expectation part, I think, has to do with imagining the possibility of feeling *sexually* to the extent that I already feel *intellectually*, am beginning to feel *emotionally.* If that has been denied you, it's hard to believe that it may actually be possible; and I've spent the last few years trying to convince myself that I could live without that kind of love. But I've been fooling myself. I don't want to die without having experienced it at least once. And I think part of what has been so frightening for me, Paula, is that on some level I knew—from the day you told me you loved me, and if I'm completely honest, probably before that—that with you it was possible.

I have no expectations of you, Paula, either sexually or

otherwise. And I hope you will try not to have any of me. All my life I've had expectations put upon me by others (of course, unless we are children, or otherwise powerless, others cannot put upon us unless we allow them to). I simply want *to be*. I want to learn to live even more fully in the present moment/in my *body*. And I think what I need from you more than from anyone else right now (making an awful lot of demands on you, aren't I? how's that for no expectations?) is the confirmation that I may simply *be*. *As* I am struggling. *As I am*.

Since September 1994, Paula and I have been together. I divorced my husband (he is a gentle and good man but one with whom I have almost nothing in common), and after a painful period for all of us, I have reestablished loving relationships with my four daughters (now ages 26 to 35). At the end of 1996, Paula and I bought an old farmhouse with two acres and a barn, where Paula has set up a sculpture and painting studio. I have a large writing room. We both work part time (Paula as a gardener and I, a writing instructor) in order to have as much time as possible for art, gardening, reading, travel, talk, and each other.

TOAST

K EDGINGTON

I snapped the latch on the dishwasher and turned to the next carton: "glasses." Outside, my parents were camouflaged in the cluster of white and bald heads that bobbed at the crest of the terrace. Getting acquainted with the residents of Sunny Grotto Retirement Village would keep the folks occupied until noon. Good. It was easier to unpack without them underfoot, bickering:

—Put the goblets on the top shelf in the rear, sherbets in front.

—Why not put the goblets where we can reach them?

—George! The china closet would look top heavy.

—Just trying to be helpful. (My father would stare at the Velcro straps of the shoes he wears since the stroke.)

—Well, you're not.

Always my mother's sense of aesthetics pitted against my father's practicality. It had been a household of uneasy compromise: the loaf of Roman Meal, its cellophane wrapper assuring freshness, resting on the silver bread plate; the *TV Guide*, not lying open on the arm of the sofa as my father wished, not tucked neatly in the brass magazine stand as my mother preferred, but placed squarely atop the most recent edition of *Smithsonian* on the lower shelf of the coffee table.

Mechanically, I stacked the dishes on the to-be-washed side of the counter, stuffed bubble wrap in one carton, and tossed Styrofoam chips in another. Forty-odd years of kitchenware to be sorted and housed in spaces seemingly too tiny to accommodate it all. In my head I arranged, then rearranged, plates, platters, salad bowls, soup tureens . . . no matter what the outcome, my mother would bitch for months.

—I can't find a damn thing. Whatever possessed that kid to stick the muffin tins over the refrigerator?

—It's not her fault; she's left-handed.

I decided the bulky stuff should go in the cupboards under the counter and searched the remaining cartons for "appliances." It was under yet another "dishes." Christ, they haven't pitched out so much as a chipped egg cup since I left home. Most of the appliances were packed in their original boxes. From "General Electric" I extracted the toaster. A single nick marred the chrome; the cloth-covered cord was discolored but not frayed.

The toaster, I realized, must be a quarter of a century old. It was surely one of the first pop-ups manufactured and had been bouncing up breakfasts for as long as I could remember, maybe even thirty years. My own toasters had perished in rapid succession. The first shorted out an entire dorm wing before meltdown. The second I lost in the divorce settlement. Number three never worked, and its replacement lasted a little over a year before it sprang its springer. Five was crushed during my most recent move, and six now dims the lights, producing pale, flaccid slices that must be coaxed from the coils with a blunt instrument.

I smiled at my distorted reflection in the GE's chrome face as phantom odors of cinnamon Pop-Tarts nudged memories of cold December mornings in the little Ohio town I no longer had reason to return to.

"Yoo-hoo! Anybody home?" The high-pitched greeting jerked me from my reverie. Stumbling through the clutter, I lurched toward the front door where, through the screen, appeared a stooped couple in flowered Bermuda shorts.

"We're the Hamiltons, Maggie and Harold. You must be a grandchild." A helmeted cake pan thrust itself forward.

"Child," I corrected, holding the toaster by its ears. The cake, Maggie, and Harold followed me into the kitchen.

"My parents are next door; they're the ones without suntans." I hoped the Hamiltons would toddle on out to join the others, but instead Maggie pressed her nose to the window to size up the newcomers.

"Harold and I just celebrated our golden anniversary. Our sons gave us a Hawaiian cruise. Three fine boys, young men, that is. Collegegraduates."

"How nice." Then recognizing a ploy to ferret out the family history, I volunteered, "My parents are approaching their forty-third."

"Oh, and you must be the youngest."

"I'm forty." I braced myself for the usual "you-certainly-don't-look-your-age" bit.

"Well, you certainly don't . . . oh, that must be your mother over by the azaleas talking with poor Mrs. Kelly . . . her husband, bless his soul, passed away last March, never sick a day, and dropped over in the living room during *Price Is Right*. That Bob Barker is my favorite. Married forty-eight years, they were, with two daughters—both divorced, such a pity these young people—and the only grandchild in Minneapolis. Now the Buckleys, they're from St. Paul—or is it Madison? Harold! Is it Madison?" Without waiting for a reply, Maggie continued to catalogue names, places, ages, and anniversaries. About halfway through the census, Harold, bless his soul, edged her politely out the back door.

After the Hamiltons' departure, I resumed toaster gazing. Someday I would inherit it, along with the eighty-three cartons of crockery and skillets. I hoped that it wouldn't be soon, that I'd have time to go through another half dozen of my own foreign-made, unrepairable toasters, toasters that seemed to have life spans as short as my relationships, equally unrepairable.

Still clutching the GE, I stared out at the denizens of Sunny Grotto, all of whom I was certain had celebrated their toasters' silver anniversaries as well as their own thirtieth, fortieth, fiftieth. No doubt every mother's heart had been broken by at least one divorced child harboring a basement full of broken appliances. To them it must seem as if something has gone terribly wrong with our generation. Planned obsolescence run amok: We had come of age in a disposable world of Pampers and Bic flashlights; for us there would be no carefully preserved packing materials in the attic; for us, two great green garbage bags by the back gate every Monday and three dozen pages of attorney listings in the metropolitan phone book, perhaps half a column under "small appliance repair."

Did they, like my mother, have nightmares of their children living in packing crates in the twenty-first century? My mother's dream flashed across the toaster: A woman both ancient and young climbs hand over hand along a frayed cord. She wears a pair of men's sneakers with Velcro straps; she's never learned to tie knots. Left-handed. The cord stretches, rhythmically negating her progress while two rows of heads, white and bald, rise alternately from the slotted top of the toaster.

On the neighbor's patio, a coffee urn gleamed in the sun, and Maggie Hamilton's cake was being divided among the villagers, their stooped shoulders steeled against a society that discards what has ceased to function, their lives soldered and epoxied against the fray.

LOUD SILENCE

CHRISTINE HALE

This winter I have done many things alone. I have been lonely, but I have learned to distinguish solitude from loneliness. A person all alone is small, but solitude is an expansive place, quiet but resonant with perception. The wind that blows there is the sound of who I am.

In December I bought a house. I found it alone, negotiated alone—no broker, no lawyer—and arrived at the closing alone. Halfway through the proceedings, the mortgage banker showed up to balance my side of the mahogany table, its glassy varnish replicating the tabletop at which a year earlier I'd negotiated my divorce settlement. That time, sick and shaking, I'd leaned on the advice of an attorney and an accountant. This time—the banker and I on one side of the table, the selling couple on the other, the closer in the middle dealing documents like hands of blackjack—I signed alone. The deed, the note, the addendum to the note. In the archaic way of real estate recordings, each one labeled me unblinkingly. *Christine Hale, a single woman.* The more papers I signed, the more secretly giddy I became at my Homeric epithet. Like the resourceful Odysseus, the appositive made me bigger than myself. I became a mission, albeit with destination unknown.

When I left the closing table, my giddiness dissolved quickly into fear about the magnitude of that unknown. A self-employed single woman with a mortgage, a single mother with a half hour to kill before picking up her children from school, I sat down on the slab patio of the rented dump where I'd served out the purgatory of separation and divorce, and I had a cigarette. I needed something forbidden. I needed tangible representation of the risk I felt myself taking in buying a house alone—an act so ordinary, at least for middle-class couples. I had a thousand things I could have been doing with those vacant minutes, but I sat smoking, dizzy with nicotine and alone under a bowl of blue Florida sky oblivious to me. How I enjoyed the hard edge that act put on me. My life looked dangerous, and from the security of that suspended moment, I decided to like it.

I like my life alone much less when I face the blank page, the empty bed, the vacuum around the dinner table when my children are with their father. Even when my children are with me and life is a spin of their activities and their needs, I often feel alone. They share with me their jokes and wishes and sorrows and fights, but as the adult, as parent-in-charge of stability, my dreams and my demons are mine. My emotional life happens in a sheath of silence. Around me there blooms a space into which I long to express myself, a space not canceled by the generous presence of my women friends, a space that seems to need a mirror, in the form of a man's face, in order for me to distinguish myself from the abyss.

No man is there. I am alone by choice, because the relationships I chose before were distorting me. Pulled this way and that—desperate to please, to know, to hold—I was nothing but strident effort.

"It is not lost on me that you have done this alone," a man said to me. A man I was pushing away, reluctantly and with what felt like suicidal bravery. I had decided, alone in one of his absences from my life, to be alone. I had clung to him for a long time, through the roiling of the divorce, needing him like air, accepting from him anything or nothing, his choice. "Alone is the lesson," I told him, denying the humility with which he offered me the words, relishing the moment of slapped silence that followed. I spoke reflexively, from the neural pathways of loss, but my words were more true than I knew. Alone was a lesson yet to be learned.

At the turn of the year, I had some surgery. On my own. Nobody there but me when the nurse read the boilerplate list of the risks. This was outpatient surgery, minor except for the general anesthesia. I knew I wasn't going to die; I knew the likelihood of experiencing more than nausea and some pain from my stitches was negligible. But when the nurse challenged me, when she told me I *would not be allowed* to go home alone in a taxi, I had a brief frisson at my audacity. She in her white-coated authority was informing me that responsible, intelligent people do not take a risk without someone who cares standing by. I lied to shut her up, telling her I'd arranged with a friend to pick me up, and when I left the pre-op, I made the lie truth by calling the friend. That little chill, I thought, had taught me something. I'd faced an abyss, seen nothing in it but other people's expectations and my own stony pride, and I was done with it. When they lowered the mask over my face on the operating table, I was loaded with tranquilizers and cool with my solitude. "Bye," I said to the doctors and the nurses, and did an existential back flip out of consciousness into the void, feeling, as I left, that these technicians' solicitude—the surgeon was stroking my immobilized palm—was dear but unnecessary.

My mind came back before my body, and that thinking self rode up from darkness on feelings—a mad in-rush of loss, every nerve screaming the memory of severed ties. Limbs paralyzed, lungs panicking against a wall of curare to seize life's breath, I was already present in the world and crying, tears springing from my eyes like arterial blood.

In mid-February I arrived in Wyoming, a sea of land such as I'd never seen—vast, bleak, frozen, and empty. I took up residence at the Ucross Foundation, everything in my life pared away to my immediate surroundings: a studio in a dish-shaped field of snow, a desk, a chair, and the blank screen of my computer, cursor blinking.

The Buddhists say it is the space inside a bell that makes the thing a bell. Without the space between clapper and cup, a bell could make no sound. Emptiness is its essence. The essence of my writing retreat was silence.

"The silence here is loud," the foundation director told me when I arrived. The first afternoon I sat in my studio, the silence pressed on my eardrums until I felt them bend inward, as if I sat on a descending plane. I was made so deaf with silence that for several days I did not hear anything except on the few occasions when people spoke to me. Then one night, walking the icy mile from the studio back to the house where I slept, I heard deer running. I heard them before I saw them, the sound pale and sibilant, more related to the flowing of water than the working of muscles and hooves. A half-dozen white-tailed deer bounded across a moonlit field, barely touching the silence, their slender legs puncturing the crusty snow like needles piercing silk.

After that night my hearing became attuned to emptiness, and I found more things to listen to. On a tiny stripped sapling I passed daily, there remained but six papery leaves. In the slightest stirring of the air, they chattered against one another. Tires on asphalt were audible long before the lone vehicle appeared. Occasionally one of the cattle bawled. Water dripped from the eaves to the porch deck when the ice loosened in noonday sun. The plastic clatter of the keys under my fingers, when I got on a writing roll, could become loud enough to distract me from my trance. And then came the wind. I sat in my studio late at night, aware that no human being was within a mile of me, and the shutters, the doors, and the roof tiles began to rattle and then to sing. I was startled and I was afraid. Not until the next morning, when the wind had died down, when I raised the window shade to view my one-tone world of snow, did I remember the Bashō haiku I had taped to the glass. I had met the wind in darkness, and its sound had neither the shape nor the effect I'd expected.

The sound of the wind, I decided, was not the noise made by air moving. What I heard when the wind blew was not the wind but the things it moved. And this told me that what I heard when I heard silence were the sounds that characterized it—the deer's hooves, desiccated leaves, the loose shingles, and finally my own fears and questions. The wind and the silence were both empty. The things I heard, and the ears I heard with, were cup and clapper of the bell. Useless, inconsequential, meaningless without the space in which to ring.

I began then to listen more carefully to my own silence, the silence in me as well as around me, finding in it not the absence of presence—*aloneness*—but the presence of what most often goes unremarked. I heard my thoughts and I heard my feelings, undistorted by my needs and others' expectations. I heard, for instance, that I wanted to write this essay, and I turned from my computer screen to my desk and began to make notes, abandoning without fear the writing of my novel, which was my business for being in retreat. I heard too, as if someone spoke these words in my ear, "I like to be by myself," and I was in no way surprised. This was not news; it was confirmation, the return of knowledge I'd possessed as a child and lost in the growing-up rush to make, and keep, connections to other people. I was, in that moment, not alone and lonely. I was present to myself.

Into the emptiness around myself, from within myself, came understandings which I recognized as my truths, given tongue by silence. The speech of solitude.

On the day before my last day in Wyoming, sated and a little bit crazed with my own company, I joined a carload of Ucross residents on a half-day's drive into Montana, to the site of what white people have been taught to call Custer's

Last Stand. The official name now is Little Bighorn Battle-field, the change a belated nod to the two-sided reality of what transpired there in 1876—for the U.S. Army, a humiliation sufficient to justify genocide in revenge, and for the Lakota and Cheyenne, a holy, Pyrrhic victory. For me, the place cried pain and repression. On all sides of the battlefield the land is the poor possession of the Crow, pocked with their souvenir stands and rusted mobile homes, but the dominant motif of the park is the tight-lipped tidiness of its U.S. military cemetery.

The day I was there was almost unbearably cold, the dark rolling wasteland limned with wind-scoured snow, the sky preparing to deliver more. I walked among acres of tombstones, among the dead from five wars, in the company of a man to whom I felt a tentative connection. We had made a tacit choice to be alone together, shedding the others who had come with us, adjusting our separate paces to allow a combination of our paths. We looked at the same things; we shared our similar responses with glances, yet we could not speak. The very presence of shared intention seemed to press speech away.

Every tombstone bore a cross, and some few had also a fluttering American flag. Puzzling out a principle that would explain the placement of the flags, uneasy in the thickening quiet between us, I had meandered some dozen steps beyond my companion when he said, "I feel like the only Jew in Montana." His words stunned me. I could meet them with nothing but embarrassed, and unbroachable, silence.

Why? I had some uncomfortable notion I should have known he was Jewish. But why should I have considered whether he was or was not that or anything else, except someone whose occasional company—over breakfast, after dinner, walking to the studios—pleased me? Yet my not-knowing, and especially my inability to say anything in response, seemed overwhelmingly important and troubling.

Driven toward the car by the stinging wind, we wound our way through the rows of identical white marble markers, searching, I thought now, for one single Star of David. We saw none. I still could not say a word to him, but during the long drive back to Wyoming, I worried over what it was we had wanted from each other, and why a need that felt so mutual resulted only in frustrated silence.

His words, lofted into the awkward, testing gap between us, seemed a brave and vulnerable effort at connection, an attempt to arc space with speech. But what we sought, I think, was not talk, not the verbal, intellectual connection we had already made over the dinner table. We wanted intimacy. We wanted the wordless content that comes from belonging, in deep knowledge and trust, to the same sphere as another human being—something each of us had too recently lost with someone else. We wanted the impossible. Our separate loneliness could not be quickly or expediently combined, and so speech failed us.

The next day, when it was time for good-bye and people gathered for the obligatory group photo, he and I leaned on each other. Shoulder to shoulder, hip to hip, for those few seconds we held each other up. In that inarticulate contact, there was mutual recognition and acceptance of our failure to join and, for me, a new lesson. Silence is both a separation and a connection. Sometimes it is the only bridge possible between two differences so distinct—between two people, or between the self and everything else.

At home now, in the house I bought, in the daily business of my life, there is noise. The noise of people and things in motion; the noise of clamoring, competing demands on my time. Even in my study—with the children in school and the phone off the hook—there is noise. Lawn mowers, barking dogs, the ticking of the clock that says writing time is almost up for today. Without silence, my self seems to fall away from me, and I am—paradoxically amid everything that involves me—alone. Lonely. I reach for solitude to comfort me, and I cannot put my hand on it. The company and clarity it granted me cannot be possessed for the asking. Emptiness cannot be grasped.

What remains is a kind of faithful seeking. An attempt to position myself at appropriate proximity and angle to what is happening around me so that connection, whether to self or others, is encouraged. When I can see my aloneness as a condition of space around myself, instead of a gulf between me and others, it ceases to deafen me. Instead of isolating and insulating me from what is around me, the space allows me to hear, to *listen* to, myself and others. What it is— this space—is a transcendence of self-absorption that permits other people and other parts of ourselves to approach. The knowledge that informs this space may or may not be spoken, but it can be heard. It comes free for the listening.

I like to sit on the porch swing at the front of my house. Summer is coming on. The mourning doves sigh in the pines, my son shoots baskets for my applause, from my daughter's room the radio blares greed and lust, there is construction under way down the street. I am forty-two years old with two children under twelve, a mortgage, erratic paying work, temporary alimony, one-third of a novel, an ex-husband with a girlfriend, an ex-boyfriend I miss but cannot call for fear I'll lose the self I've barely found. One missed connection after another.

Sometimes I light a cigarette. My children disapprove, and they are right. Nicotine is a drug; it teaches me nothing. Better to sit in the swing and listen. Between the sounds are spaces. The doves sometimes fall silent, hammers are laid down, the children come and sit beside me. Sometimes it is so quiet I can hear who I am, and then who I might be in different circumstances does not matter. From this solitary place, I can touch what is.

RUNNING WOMAN

. . . SHE WASN'T REALLY VERY GOOD AT LIFE.
THEN AGAIN: NEITHER WERE LAUREL AND HARDY.
— *Kurt Vonnegut*

TRICIA LANDE

I lay half folded like one of those fossilized women anthropologists find in stone crypts in Turkey or South America or somewhere. They always look to me like they'd been cut down in the act of running, one knee raised just higher than the other, dropped over sideways with bits of their lives: jugs, utensils, pieces of leather goods, what have you, thrown in next to them. I wasn't in a stone crypt of course, but in the hawthorn bushes that hugged the side of my California bungalow, where I waited for a thief.

My feet hurt. They always hurt. So I sat up and took my shoes off, set them beside my head, and lay back down. I half dozed, half listened, and entertained a certain unsureness about what the hell I was doing.

Burned out. Menopausal. Feeling mad. Pushing the envelope. My husband, Herb, says these things about me.

Oh baby, if you could see me now. That envelope, the big square brown kind, has been pushed all the way through the slot.

I keep telling him I just want to sell, run, get out while we're still young enough to read a road map and go to the toilet unassisted. Maybe buy a little place out in the high desert where there are no people, maybe no phones, and do . . . something.

"Like what?" Herb says. "Learn the piano? Play the *Goldberg Variations*? Weave tapestries in muted colors of hunting hounds and dead pheasants? Break bricks with our feet?"

Then our only child, the kid, the boy, the wonderson, drops out of college and moves to Mojave. He has a job where he wears a shirt with his name monogrammed across his left breast. *Donny.* Not *Donald.* Not *Don. Donny,* for heaven's sake. Hadn't I read him *Goodnight Moon? Peter Pan* —not the Disney version but the original—and Dickens? I had read Dickens to him. Now he works at a Mojave gas station. These were the big mud holes I'd waded around, made it through, risen above. But the small ones, the foot-size cavities, they were taking some talking down.

For example: Herb's clock collection. He started that collection after he'd lost his job of nineteen years. He'd lost his job because he was fifty-three and that's the truth, although there is no way to really prove such things. Downsizing, they call it. The only downsize involved was the salary of the twenty-five-year-old who replaced him, downsized to half of what Herb had made. Herb feels less than what he has been. Understandable. He works as hard as ever looking for a job, and between interviews he collects and fixes old clocks. Not understandable.

Herb started with a black cat clock straight out of the '50s. He found it at a yard sale, and it has rhinestones in a tail that moves back and forth, as do the white eyes in its ugly pinched face. From there things have escalated to brown cows, black crows, red chickens, and a large pink hog with one eye that winks luridly with every tock. Herb insists it's a pig, but it's a hog. The difference being that a hog is a sexually mature pig, and this creature looks pretty damned mature to me. When Herb finishes fixing a clock, he hangs it on the kitchen wall.

Sometimes when I'm alone in the kitchen, with all that ticking, all that time slowly lost and gone in one room, the image of my stepfather right before he died comes to me. The old man had found a station on his band radio where he could hear the atomic clock tick. He was pleased that he could know with exact certainty what time it really was. Time set by some universal standard. So he listened to that clock tick away the remains of his life while staring at a blank TV screen. I myself prefer staring at the dryer, all those colors rotating around and around. Reds, yellows, blues that fade to green. Fade to black.

Another reason to run: urban wildlife. Two months before Herb lost his job, we bought a house in Long Beach. A straight shot up the 710 Freeway to the University Medical Center near downtown L.A. where I'm an administrator. One freeway. Well, two if you count that short stretch on the Santa Monica. Easy driving.

"A real classic," the real estate agent had said. Three weeks after we moved in, the hot-water heater upped and died in the middle of my shower, and the ceiling fan in the living room landed in the center of the coffee table. It seems the urban wildlife, roof rats (attic rats, really) had eaten through the wiring. The cat had eaten a number of the rats and puked on my best pair of shoes. Rich food doesn't agree with Dave.

The list goes on. However, the final straw, the broken camel's back, the grasping crevice that had firmly wedged my foot came about because somebody—another member of the urban wildlife grouping—was stealing my greenery off my screened porch. It started with a modest asparagus fern in a plastic pot, then impatiens in yellow ceramic. Finally, he'd walked off with lilies of the Nile in a terra-cotta crock. Soon the area would be cleared, empty, and I would not allow that. I would nail the scumbag. I would.

"The thing to understand," I told Herb after one of his comments regarding menopausal madness, "is that none of this has anything to do with your job, or Donald, any more than the house has to do with Dave puking. Shit happens. You just have to work a little harder for control."

I'd nearly caught the thief when he stole the impatiens.

I'd seen him through my front window as he took the steps two at a time. I knew the type. One of the Underpass People who live next to the freeway. The kind who hear bumps in the night and decide these bumps are signs from God. Or a Donald Trump bump directing him to steal front porch plants as protection from outer space beams. Sick people. People who live in bushes. People who can no longer function.

Look, I know these people face bigger mud holes than I do every day. And I know most of them were once something else: lawyers, cab drivers, used car salesmen. Once they were kids. Kids don't dream of living under the freeway, or of being used car salesmen. Or of being hospital administrators, for that matter. I didn't say: Mom, someday I'm going to be an administrator. I want a desk and a chair and a door with a Do Not Disturb sign that people routinely ignore when they storm into my office wearing white lab coats (yes, okay, with their names monogrammed over their left breast) and say, "I need more money for my research project," or "Why the hell can't that receptionist make decent coffee, for chrissake?"

No, I wanted to be a writer, touch people's lives, leave an imprint that says: Hey, I was on the planet for a minute there. I wanted to go to parties where people wore Birkenstocks and beige and talked about French literature in rooms with rosewood paneling. Instead I move paper from one side of my desk to the other. I've got a *real* job. People said that to me back then: "You've got to get a *real* job."

Okay. Chase scene number one: So this plant thief wore army fatigue pants and a ribbed T-shirt cut between his thin white shoulder blades that pumped in alternate rhythm when he ran. When I chased after.

I was nearly there, an arm's length away. He was smaller than me, shorter anyway. I could take him down, take control. No more shit happening. That would be the end of that.

But I tripped. I fell hard, and the asphalt took a length of skin off my arm. I stayed there in the street and gritted my teeth because I knew, in that one blinding second, that it was the way I would die—a little old lady tripping over a root, a rock, Dave. I'll go down someday and break a hip. They'll call Donny and he'll come—looking sad and wearing that damned shirt. I'll spend weeks in a nursing home smelling Pine Sol and old people's piss, then go out with pneumonia. My gravestone will read: *What's-Her-Name. She moved papers.*

That was how it had gone last time. I had tripped. This time, chase scene number two would be a different story. These were my thoughts as I dozed off behind the hawthorns.

Yellowstone. I danced around the edges of the mud pots, created by an ancient volcanic upheaval that lay just beneath the surface of the earth. The air smelled of hot dirt and sulfur; I stuck a foot into the ooze. The mud was soft, warm, and squeezed between my toes. A bubble the size of a bread loaf boiled up, popped, imploded in on itself, leaving a hole. Another bubble, larger than the first, exploded. No, not exploded. Slammed. Slammed like a door. A screen door. My screen door.

I awoke. It took a second. Nobody was on the porch, and neither was the wooden park bench I'd just bought at Home Depot.

I lurched through the hawthorn bushes and caught my sweatshirt sleeve on a branch, pulled loose, staggered out, and came around the side of my neighbor's house just as he crouched out of his front door in his Fruit of the Looms. Charlie reached for his newspaper and froze, hunched. We looked at each other.

"My bench is gone," I said.

"Oh," Charlie said.

"Dirtbag!" I shouted.

"Hey, I was only going for my paper. I wasn't . . ."

"Stop him!" I was off.

Up the block, just turning the corner, the guy dressed in army fatigues and red tennis shoes pushed a shopping cart with the bench balanced across the top.

I was on the move. Running. Rain came down—when had that started? Oil floated on the street, iridescent green like the back of a Japanese beetle. Asphalt dug into my bare feet. Slap, slap, slap.

My peripheral vision is good. "Good for a woman your age," my doctor had said. It allows me a broadside view of the world. There was Charlie, still slightly hunched, a plump gnome with his paper, the surface of Charlie's picture window reflecting a tall, skinny, shoeless, middle-aged woman in a purple sweat suit running. Running for all she was worth.

III

Re-creation

YOU NEED ONLY TO CLAIM THE EVENTS OF YOUR LIFE

TO MAKE YOURSELF YOURS. WHEN YOU TRULY POSSESS

ALL YOU HAVE BEEN AND DONE, WHICH MAY TAKE

SOME TIME, YOU ARE FIERCE WITH REALITY.

—*Florida Scott-Maxwell*

SEEING STARS

MARY ANNE MAIER

Jane and I play makeup. It makes me feel cool, a little crazy, cheeky, like we're getting away with something. I want to tell people *See? We're a lot of fun, Jane and I. We have a wild streak. We're sharing the mysteries of womanhood. We're not afraid to admit to our secret yearnings. I mean we're out there— absolutely* edgy.

All of this brought on by cosmetology, you understand. (The word makes me see stars every time.) The truth is that I only pretend to know about makeup in our sessions; I'm actually a rank novice. It's what comes of being a girl in the '60s and early '70s, that time of shiny new possibilities for our half, of hopes hardening into expectations quicker than some of us could find a form that really fit. Girls suddenly had to prove they could go on to do anything. Astronauts, senators—sure. But putting on makeup, doing hair, painting nails were not among the acceptable anythings, even on the side. We were way too smart for such drivel, and besides, we didn't need to paint ourselves up like the Barbies we'd so recently forsaken in some ridiculous attempt to please men.

Still, I thought Jane, my older and more cosmopolitan sister, must have picked up a fair compendium of cosmetological insights over the years, probably through osmosis since it would be some kind of mortal sin for a woman of her intellect to study something that shallow. But it ends up that she never got far beyond me on this particular learning curve. So we're left dabbling in the secret art together now, the way others might experiment with witchcraft. Our Witchy Witchy Red nails. Our Bewitching Bronze eyeshadow.

We didn't even get going on this secret dalliance until my sister was in her late thirties, forties, so I was early thirties and on through. Very slow start. For one thing, we hardly ever see each other. We meet at the folks' house if I come home from out of state and she can get away to drive the couple hundred miles of wilderness separating her from them. It's really no easier for her to drive hours across the state than it is for me to fly in, I know, but if I flew in and borrowed a car to go up and see her, we'd never play makeup. That's just a given. It's something we do only at our parents' house. Not that this is *why* we get together at all; it's just one of those patterns you fall into, like maybe you drink iced tea and eat those little packages of cheese crackers (which come in zesty salsa now, by the way) when you go on a road trip.

So we decide, say the afternoon she arrives or the first morning we're both there together, that we'll play makeup. Later in the day, then, we go out for something, maybe something to make for dinner, and that's when we stock up. We hardly ever go even to the drugstore, though, and never, ever to a cosmetics counter. (Too public? Taking the whole thing too damn seriously?) We simply peruse the brash brands they sell at the supermarket a couple of blocks from our parents' place: Maybelline, Cover Girl, Revlon, Sally Hansen, L'Oréal. Cheap cheap cheap. Because we're worth it. No-name glue-on nails with big, thick emery boards to shape them. Lipstick with extra shine and nail polish that's frosted. Once we bought Sun-In for our hair. One thing usually leads to another: Liquid makeup demands pressed powder—that's not even news to us. But how about those foam wedges for applying the foundation, for blending artfully? How about the lip smoother to keep our lipstick from feathering into the fine lines that threaten our lip boundaries? We're under the spell of delicate scents that call up

subliminal connections with other women we love or respect, of alluring packaging that melts us into hopeful adolescence somewhere deep—a place we've dreamed of melt-
ing for thirty years now.

I'm certain that touch is part of it: How long since
someone traced my jawline with an index finger like a
feather, awe in his eyes, the way Michael Douglas does to
every leading woman? (I've had just instants of coveting
blindness to make touch a necessity.) Maybe you have to be
twenty-three for that to happen to you as a woman, while
Michael Douglas cruises along blithely at thirty-three, then
forty-three, fifty-three, his female leads hovering motion-
less, like whirring hummingbirds. But of course that's not
true: No one out-whirs time; they're traded in. Anyway,
touch is an essential, an es-*sensual*, an ache, from birth to the
tender brow-mopping that we hope accompanies our last
breath, and yet we pretty much run out of reasons for people
to touch us in other-than-sexual ways when we're about
eight. There's that groping period for a few teen years that
can be very good or very bad, but adult sex doesn't demand
much intentional touch at all. This has to be half the reason
hair salons and makeup counters and massage therapists and
chiropractors have such enormous success in our culture,
and movies, too—the former allowing us to experience
sanctioned touch that is both delicate and serious (oh, how
we ache!), while the latter lets our longings be assuaged
through spirit travel into the waiting arms on screen, tuck-
ing ourselves right in front of Gwyneth Paltrow to catch
Michael Douglas's soft-gliding touch on our own now-
firm, now-twenty-three-year-old jawline.

For Jane and me, playing makeup gives us powers unknown to us in real life. It's playing Superman with a twist.
(Wonder Woman, created to be inherently less than Superman, would never do. Besides, just look at her tastelessly
thick eyeliner and those ridiculous fake lashes!) When we
step into the phone booth, we change from the strong and

rational to the smooth and intuitive—mild mannered, if you will. In everyday life, two professional women prove to the world they can be as hard-driving as any man around. But when they play makeup, one becomes a cosmetologist possessing unfathomable stores of intuitive understanding about the enchanting properties of cosmetics, a woman who devotes her life not to brainy superpowers but to enhancing touch through the creative application of mystical products. The other, then, is the kind of woman with time on her hands, money to burn, and plump, luscious, touchable skin. I think of Cleopatra moving slowly, exquisitely through each honey-thick moment, never letting on under those weighty eyelids that she's ready to strike like a cobra. I try to imagine both of us verdant with lush intuitive powers—so unlike our other selves that we're even capable of *sssslllllinking*, of napping voluptuously, of losing control—I mean *letting go utterly*.

This is usually in the late afternoon when Dad's still at work or otherwise occupied and Mom is busy around the house, or at night after Dad's asleep. There's no rule or anything, but it seems best this way. We begin by washing our faces. The cosmetologist then smooths rich, creamy moisturizer into the leisure-class woman's neck and face, dabbing the lotion around at first (I learned this from Jane) and then moving into upward neck strokes, heel-of-the-hand lifts from the jawline, tiny circular three-finger rubs on the cheeks, tender finger pats below the eyes, and upward-outward massage of the eyebrows and forehead, with circles again for the temples. (I wonder sometimes if Jane picked up some of these techniques from expensive facials, maybe massages she's had but doesn't want to tell me about.)

As we take turns in these roles, the student threatening to sue the university where Jane's an administrator dwindles to dust behind her gorgeously highlighted brown eyes, sculpted with Soft Mocha pencil liner and Fawn Brown mascara, the dark circles under her eyes now faded to sultry with just enough Early Dawn fair concealer. And for me, the problem of missing Record Group numbers in the National Archives citations of the book I'm editing becomes as obscure an issue as it is to the rest of the world, and Peachy-Plum blush is the key: It's as if I have a natural glow from within.

We relax into the ritual, relishing the scents and senses, but I have to admit that we never really lose control. Instead of sinking into intuitive pools of being, we're careful to act exceedingly smug about what we're doing. —*Shall we edit your nail color, dear? Just polish it up a bit? I'm thinking specifically of Midnight Magic. —Certainly, Dr. Manacurski. You're the sorceress here; I put my hands in your hands.* We speculate about how anyone could spend her life concerned with the physical, the concrete (*Can you imagine?*), as if the abstract constructs with which we occupy our days are of immeasurably greater importance to the world. I tell Jane about all the eighteen-year-olds crammed into every women's room at a community college within walking distance of the Mexican border where I used to teach. These students fought for mirror space and electrical outlets every day, producing hair dryers, jumbo cans of spray, even hot rollers from backpacks. I always assumed the primary difference between them and me was not age but priorities: Even at eighteen, I carried only books in my backpack. I say all this to remind us both that we only play at cosmetology rather that living by it, to make clear we don't need this simple diversion. But it hits me, as I picture those young women, how nearly my desperation mirrors theirs, my straining for attention simply taking the form of papers I've written, books I've edited. (Oh, lord, how frightfully we ache.)

As for doing cosmetology professionally, it's true I couldn't stand to touch strangers' hair or skin; the thought repulses me. (In my defense, or perhaps cosmetology's, medicine would evoke the same response from me.) And I bet the chemicals beauticians handle all day kill brain cells like crazy. Yet on a scale of realness, even utility, I wonder seriously if cosmetology doesn't stand right up there next to a good bit of the academic work done today, let alone current therapeutic efforts. I had the experience, for example, of going to a hairdresser for a cut in the midst of a flat, white-gray depression. She took one look at me and knew immediately that I should get my hair highlighted to improve my mood. "It'll give you a boost, hon," she said, and she was absolutely right. So much better than a therapist—almost a shaman, really. One session and I could catch respectable semigloss highlights reflecting from my eyes for a couple of weeks afterward. I never say it to Jane, of course, but I sometimes think people like us go to school forever to shield ourselves from such easy relief, from human touch and our own mirrored image, from wild possibilities with names like Delta Dawn Dreams and Tattletale Taupe.

Once, before our mother died, she came in the big bathroom to put away towels she'd folded, still warm from the dryer. It was my turn to be done, to be the pampered leisure-class woman, but we asked Mom if she wanted to play. She chuckled at the silliness before resting gratefully on the toilet seat to receive the royal treatment: the extended moisture massage followed by Nude-Nude foundation blended with the use of our new foam wedges, Cinnamon Cappuccino blush adding drama to her cheekbones. Autumn Heather shadow warmed her drooping lids, with Bright Moonbeams below the eyebrows giving her a lift. It was the touch, of course—she had a hard time keeping her eyes half open as I held my breath to brush on mascara and Jane curled her lashes with the little scissor-handled device created just for that purpose. We gave her a more muted, wet lip color than she was used to (Copper Sizzle) and used the feathery touch of a cosmetics brush to set the whole look with a little pressed powder. After we'd puffed up her hair and sprayed it into place, we gave her back her glasses so she could discover herself in the mirror and savor that satisfying reflected glow, that sense of enchantment created every time by this cosmetological mingling of memory and hope. Then, on a whim, we paraded her out to the family room to show her off to Dad.

He couldn't tell the difference, couldn't figure out what he was supposed to see, and I felt her radiance melt into pulsating nervous heat as she stood on display. Had he stopped seeing her thirty years before, just as I felt myself fading now from the eyes of my husband, the plumber, the baggers at the grocery store? Jane and I tried to fill the dead space, mumbled something about feminine mystique, but we all knew what scene had just been replayed for the billionth time in human history: She was still there, her real self still inside, longing to feel the thrilling burn of his searing eyes once more or the tender glide of a finger along her soft, sagging jawline. Yet our charms and spells, so potent in their stirrings of youth and yearnings, of dreams and daring, are powerless before those not possessing our X-ray vision, unable to see the spark reignited by our beautifying touch as a tiny, hope-filled star-glow within our souls. We three women knew right then that there wasn't enough Copper Sizzle in the galaxy to make us visible again to men in these, our invisible years. For the billionth time in human history, we took it personally. How else?

How else when we see each other now with such clarity that it chokes my heart sometimes and I have to gasp? When these forays into cosmetology bring us back into a gentle, touching focus even in our own eyes? Perhaps this is where our real magic lies: Our imaginations are large enough to hold more than our own image. We know Gloria Steinem and Carolyn Heilbrun are absolutely right—our lives are much, much more than existence in the fickle gaze of mere men. Yes, of course, of course. But that's not our purpose here, or our pain, exactly, though having the light we've conjured reflect back to us as not only not-light, but not-being, is an ache that reaches beyond the sensual to the essence. Essence-tial.

And yet, as all women, we will continue. We will continue. In the end, I'm certain this ritual of being will blend ever so artfully with our dreams, our days. (We'll consider the slightest variation of tone, of tender hue, as elemental in the changing light.) *Remember, woman, you are dust and to dust you shall return.* Probably. Star Dust, Dream Dust, Delicate Dusty Rose. No doubt we'll return to all of them before it's over.

COME TO THE WINDOW

DIANE ACKERMAN

So many selves make up a life, especially the early parts of one's life. Shouldn't there be a statute of limitations on guilt? "I am no longer responsible for acts committed by my previous selves" is a motto I sometimes wish we could live by. Selves will accumulate when one isn't looking, and they don't always act wisely or well. This was not what I expected when I was a child growing up in the Midwest, where the snows were shoulder high, piles of leaves could be dived into, and my life shone before me as a clear trajectory. It was the fairy tale I had been told to expect: A Knight in Shining Armor would appear suddenly to guide me and heal my life, then I would produce two children, buy a dog, work at a pleasant job, and live forever in an oasis of calm. An invisible boarder in my house, a fantasy friend became my confidante. I sometimes gossiped with her about the bohemian lives of artists; but I never dreamed that I would grow up to live such a life myself. It is only now, in my middle years, that I've begun to notice how my selves have been forming layer upon layer, translucent as skin; and, like skin, they are evolving a certain identifiable "fingerprint"—a weather system of highs and lows, loops and whirls.

Yes, I think, as I pull back the thick rind on an orange, feeling the zest release a fine spray of juice over my cheeks and nose, my caravan of selves probably began when I was little, inventing mental adventures in which I starred. My daily life was unbearable. I could have run away, I suppose,

but instead I fled mentally along the Silk Road of the imagination. One continuing fantasy was that I was not human
but an extraterrestrial, part of a group of itinerant artists
who traveled throughout the universe. On their planet, art
was deeply revered and prized, and above all, they relished
discovering the arts of various life-forms, because it revealed
so much about hearts and needs, values and yearnings. Each
itinerant artist was born into the civilization of a planet and
grew up soul-drenchingly creative, remembering nothing
of the planet of origin. As one of those artists, my job was
to feel. And so I felt, penetratingly, exaltingly, agonizingly.
I peered for long hours into the hidden recesses of things. I
trotted after thoughts to see where they led. And, in time, I
created a beautiful sampler of the range of human feeling
and experience. Then, toward what I naturally imagined to
be the end of my life, I one day heard a voice saying to me:
"Come to the window. The night air is sweet. . . ."

Decoyed by the simple beauty of the evening, I went to
the window, inhaled the scent of jasmine drifting in, and
was suddenly amazed to see an alien standing there. All at
once my mission became clear to me; I knew my work was
done on Earth, that my destiny was to rest awhile on the
small city-state of the mother ship, and then be born on a
new planet, into another species, to undergo extremes of
feeling and create art from that amalgam of privilege and or-
deal. Learning I was not human shocked and saddened me,
and I begged to be allowed to remain human. The separation was grueling. Humans were among the most emotional
and volatile of all the planetarians in the universe, but human was what I knew and loved, and I could not bear the
thought of leaving Earth, leaving with so much still unex-
plored and unvoiced. "It is enough," I was assured. "There
are other worlds to explore, other beings to become." And
so I went with the alien to the spaceship beyond Earth's or-
bit, and rejoined my troupe of artists, some of whom were
also between lives. That otherworldly dream haunted my

early years and adolescence, and I half expected that one day I really would be summoned to the hidden part of my destiny with a whisper: "Come to the window. The night air is sweet. . . ."

As I grew older, what I craved was to be ten or twelve selves, each passionately committed to a different field—to be a dancer, a surgeon, a carpenter, a composer, an astronaut, a psychologist, a brain chemist, an ice skater. Some would be male, some female, and all of their sensations would feed back to one central source. Surely then I would begin to understand the huge spill of life, if I could perceive it from different viewpoints, through simultaneous lives. I had been writing creatively since I could write. If I couldn't actually live simultaneous lives, perhaps I could do so serially—by giving myself passionately, blood and bones, to what I wrote about, by becoming my subjects.

My most recent self lives in a small town of trees, waterfalls, and flowers, where most people know or at least recognize one another, and many of their stories converge. From time to time, I travel to distant places in pursuit of the marvelous. But, after all, the marvelous is a weed species; it thrives everywhere, even in yards and ditches. So I always return home to friends and loved ones. Through the many windows of a house in the woods, I watch the doings of the deer, squirrels, and birds, and the metamorphosing seasons. I think a lot about the pageant of being human—what it senses, loves, suffers, thrills to—while working silently in a small room, filling blank sheets of paper. It is a solitary mania. But there are still times when, all alone, I could be arrested for unlawful assembly.

SHARING A ROOM

B ETH K EPHART

The father of her seventh child has not yet come, and she is large with anger—seems to fill the bed, seems to hammer it deeper into the pale white hospital floor whenever she turns or even sighs. When she talks, the bed sinks deeper. When she tells me what she must tell me, the sound is like a clenched fist falling: *This child, I didn't want it; she so ornery; wouldn't come out, 'cept with a knife. And they're giving me till three, this my fourth day here, and he don't come, they say they'll call me a cab, they say that, and I say, Don't have cab money, no cab fare, didn't bring it, didn't plan on this; I thought this bastard would be different from the rest. Thought, This time. Thought, Finally.* She has been lying on her back, her knees poked skyward, but now she lets her legs bang down, one and then the other. Above her bed, the tent of her sheet slops aimlessly around in the air, then bumbles and plummets too, confused.

We met in the dark, past midnight. The nurses were quiet as they conveyed me to this room, and their fingers never bothered with the light. My parents were gone, and so was my husband; my son, exhausted from a too-long journey into life, was sporting a new striped hat beneath the nursery neon. If I had to have something, I was told, then use the buzzer. Otherwise, one nurse told me sternly, I'd be smart to sleep. You don't know it now, but this is your last night of mercy, she offered, and I was given all the aids of comfort, then left alone in the shadows.

But not alone. I was too dazed and elated to have seen it before, but I was sharing a room with another. Beyond my own partly rent screen, behind a second pair of draperies, she was lying there, awake. This is an odd-shaped room, a chunk of which is missing, and so the beds, where I lie, aren't side by side, but directly across from each other—her feet near my feet, our heads against opposite walls. Last night, I was only wanting to recover my body when I heard the second pair of curtains thrown apart. I could see the figure on the bed well enough despite the darkness, and my heart groaned in my chest.

She maunders on. She talks, and I can smell her cigarette breath all the way over here, the putrescent air she speaks with, though by now it must be three days at least since she last sucked the nicotine down. With the dawn, I can see her more clearly—the loosened braids around her head, the broken teeth in her spotted gums. I can see whatever the sheets don't hide, whatever the too-small orange nightshirt seems to desperately disclose. I am aware that I am ugly, too, that I am a sin for sore eyes—the ravaged evidence of thirty-six hours of labor and then this complication of another woman's wrath, her inexhaustible rage, her unbelievable situation: The father of her seventh child has not come to see her through. *I made him lucky*, my roommate keeps saying. *I was his dreamboat girl. He was the one, he drove me here, he said, I'll park the car and be back soon. I promise. He says that, I wait, I sit in that lobby, I walk round and around in that lobby, all those striped chairs? I walked around. I tell everyone my man's coming for me, you'll see, this man's the real thing, and then it's too late, I'm leaking water all over the rug, that fancy carpet, and this girl, she don't cooperate, and my man, he don't come like the parking lot's full, and then they say, the doctors say, that everything's backwards so they cut me apart. Like I was meat or something. Like I was.* Only once has the other world come through our door, a nurse to check on me, and when this happened, my roommate fell silent, as if she'd gone to sleep. I had wanted to whisper something to the nurse, send her a sign, tell her, Rescue me, but I couldn't because of Barbara. Another woman. Another time.

Many years ago, I was twenty-six and newly married, and it was winter. Though it was cold enough for snow, rain was falling, a gray slush in a steel city that my husband and I tramped through—one umbrella, a thin suitcase, a magazine held between us, did we also hold hands? When we reached the hospital, we stopped on the black rubber mats and watched the glass doors slide apart, and after that we began obeying all the signs. It seemed grayer inside than out, much colder; the air was a film that was difficult to see through.

At the front desk, my husband asked all the questions and confirmed the arrangements, took care of things. Already I could not talk—not in the way I would not be talking the next day and for months to follow (the bones in my chin and jaw replaced with steel, bolts, wire; my teeth wired intricately shut), but in the way I can never talk when I am frightened, undone by an imagination that insists on itself and will not demur. My husband led me down the gray-steeped hallways and in and out of sampling rooms. He assisted with the bracelet. He wore my coat on the hanger of his shoulder and arm. He carried my suitcase, my ridiculous magazine. I was a few steps behind him when we reached the last room in that series of rooms, the place where I was to anticipate an operation, and then emerge from one.

When he saw what was waiting for me, my husband stopped and looked back. With his slender body, he tried to fill the door frame, to screen the other side from view. *I love you*, he said. *This will all be over soon.* I nodded. I pushed past him. I thought rapaciously of lying down under all that gray air and being alone, and that's when I met Barbara. She had the bed against the window. She was shocking. She was crooked, a cripple. She was deformed.

No. That isn't right. Barbara was not deformed. She was

towering, she was filthy, she was half undressed, she was battered. The whole side of her face, I learned later, had been
cudgeled senseless by the butt of a gun. She worked a bar on
one of the meanest streets in Philadelphia, and walking
home late one night to whomever was the boyfriend then,
to the thirteen-year-old daughter, to the one-year-old
grandson, Barbara was jumped and robbed for her fifteen
dollars, and then beaten for good measure—her teeth stumbling out of her mouth, the hinge of her jaw broken into
threes. Barbara, when I met her, was two days past her surgery, and one side of her face was pinned with steel while
the other was hopelessly toothless. Her daughter was with
her, and her infant grandson, and when my husband and I
appeared at the doorway, all of them turned at once. Barbara, her words made hollow and twisted by the bars of steel
in her mouth, hollered hello. My husband said hello. I tried
to speak but could not. I tried to say, There must be some
mistake.

It is beside the point of this story to tell all that happened
next. What matters is that I lay in my hospital bed that night
with two separate but equally powerful fears: the fear of a
grueling, complex operation; the fear of the woman, brack-
ish and grotesque, who was sharing my room. If you had
asked me then what I was most afraid of, I would have said,
I am not safe.

But dawn came, and the needles, and the cot they roll
you away in, and when you are flat on your back like that,
you don't see the gray air; you see the yellow, acidic lights,
the fixtures in the ceilings that mask the time of day. You see
the faces, fractions of the doctors you've been consulting for
over a year; you feel the cold fit of a catheter; you see the
tubes they will be sliding down your nose and the buckets
they'll use to catch your escaped fluids, your blood. You hear
somebody say, *We're finally going to get that mouth right, Beth.
We're going to fix that jaw. You'll be able to chew again, eat real
food, now what do you think about that?* You hear somebody

counting backward above your head, and when you wake again, you thrash once, then thrash twice in the prison of your body, in the terror of what you have resurfaced to: Your mouth clamped wholly and airlessly shut, your face pulpy as fruit, the tubes in your nose obstructing the air that you must breathe; you must get a swallow of air. Then you are wheeled back into your room, and you notice, from the one window you are able to find with your frantic eyes, your hardly apprehending eyes, that it is dark outside; not dawn, but night. And still you must tell someone that you cannot breathe, but there is no way to speak, and even your hands are mute at your side. When they lift you, from one wheeled bed to another, you see, it's true, that you have gone from white to red, that blood is the color of jewelry, melted rubies. It's like a sheet on you now, it becomes your bed. And now you are slipping beneath the sea of red, and now there are hands all around you, enclosing you, mopping you, correcting the tubes, saying, *We're pumping the blood from your stomach now. This is a machine. This is how it works.* Somewhere in the room, someone asks a question and the voice comes back. *It was harder than we planned for. We've lost a lot of blood.* You don't understand. You have no way of declaring your confusion, your disgust at your own seeping vulnerability. But then you know that your family is near, and your husband, monitoring the pumps and tubes, smoothing the fresh sheets down, talking to you softly, taking care.

They allowed my husband to stay until midnight. It being near Christmas, the hospital was short staffed, and the nurses were glad for the extra pair of hands, for someone to supervise the machine that kept clogging, kept sending the blood in wrong directions, red gash across my chin, red gash upon the pillow; how many fresh pillowcases did my husband bring me that night? From across the curtains, Barbara said that she could help too, that she had had the same funked machine stuffed down her gut and she knew just how it worked, she was good at it, she was proud, in fact, that she was so good at that machine. Then the nurse came for my husband and said that it was time for him to go, that everything was okay now; the worst was over, the machine was running well. *I'll be back,* my husband promised, and when he rose and left the room, it was just me and Barbara and the hour of night, with Barbara declaring that she'd been watching the skies, and that the rain had finally turned into snow. *Hot damn, girl, look over here and watch the snow.*

Had I even wanted to, I could not comment back. Nor could I gesture, nor bring myself to turn my head, to find solace in either Barbara or her snow. I was afraid of not breathing, afraid of the laboring pump at my head, afraid of Barbara, and I kept my eyes trained on the crack of light beneath the door, as if that were the key to my safety. On the other side of me, Barbara continued her blather, asking me questions, offering stories, chronicling her bar, her men, her thirteen-year-old Liz, who last year, Barbara swore to it, got an A in math at school. Barbara spoke with a tongue loose in her head. She was careless with vowels, she scraped the edge off her words. Entire sentences slapped against the metal bars that held her fractures in one place, so that what she said either doubled back or was diffused. But Barbara talked, and Barbara talked, unbothered by the sound of her own voice, immune to my silence, my thoughts.

How late did it get? How much snow fell that evening? I can't remember closing my eyes, but I will never forget reawakening. Something was wrong with the machine. It had clogged, more than the usual clog; it seemed broken. The blood had stopped moving through the plastic tubes in my nose, and my jaw was fist tight, and I was drowning, and I knew it, and I couldn't say so. There was a buzzer by my hand. I reached and pressed it. Ripped a needle out of my arm as I stabbed the green button over and over, and waited for help to come, give me a nurse, give me a well-dressed nurse from the opposite side of the world.

But nothing happened. The acrid bar of light beneath

the door was never splintered, never pierced by the clean white shoes of nurses, calming voices, hands that could set the thing right. I was aware of the blood in my body oozing to all the wrong places, of my lungs going flat, without air. I was aware of my vision growing brighter—of patterns and pictures, odd shapes, geometries, my husband's face, my mother's, an apology I'd never made, something that belonged to my sister. I was aware that I was dying, and that there was nothing left to me but to watch the show of memories in my mind, and I gave up on the buzzer then, and I gave up on life.

But when I woke again, the world was Barbara. Everything was Barbara, her hot terrible breath above me, her roughened hands below me, her misshapen words saying, *I got you, I got this damned machine too. Damn machine. You nearly died on me, girl. You nearly slapped this bed silly.* Barbara with her hospital gown undone and her naked body lurched forward, Barbara sitting on my bed beside me, and me half naked too, both of us that close, and me in the arms of her safety. I couldn't speak, I could not say a word, and not because of the wires and the rubber and the bolts inside my head, not because of the tubes, now slowly unclogging, but because of the shame that filled my heart, the truth that I woke to: that for no good reason I had managed to give her, Barbara had left her world and rescued mine.

Jeremy was conceived two years later, a night of rain, a night of perfect clarity between my husband and me. There were things I wanted to tell him, and that night I could, that night the sound of the rain was the sound of truth falling: quiet confessions, hidden shames. I told my husband about Barbara, how I had behaved in his absence—so full of disrespect and disdain, so certain that my life depended on the yellow light and the cold gray hall beyond my door, and not on the gentle snow Barbara invited me to see. *Turn your head, you'll see.* I told my husband that it was true, what people say, that when you die your life ticks backward, and when you wake, miraculously, again, your heart is the only organ you can speak through. I told my husband that I believed in life, that I wanted to create and touch it, that I wanted to teach my child, our child, the lessons of my life.

I do not know the name of the woman who lies across from me now; she's never said. I know her smells. I know her story. I know the sound of the bed twisting beneath her fury. I know the attack of her envy, because soon the nurse will bring me my son, and he won't be ornery, and he'll have a father who will be there, who will hold him, who will love him, outrageously, his whole life long. I know that there is a line drawn down this room, and on one side lies joy and on the other, sorrow; something healed, at last, and something broken. And beside the spectacle of dawn, beside the shuffle of the coming crepe-soled shoes, there is a trace of Barbara too, her hands beneath my head, her mangled language saying clear as day, *Turn your head, girl. I ain't no stranger. Turn your head, so you'll see.*

MIGRATION OF THE HEART

D E B O R A H F R U I N

The vineyards around my house are filled with starlings in
the throes of winter migration, tugged southward the way
the tide is at the mercy of the moon. They show up a few at
a time late in autumn, gather, rise up and fall upon the vines,
feasting on the few grapes left after harvest. When they take
flight en masse, all you can hear is the beating of wings.

The stir is echoed by the beating of my heart, restless and
trembling, rising and falling, taking my poise away. The
place I stand, the road I travel are bathed in the holy light of
the year's end, in air perfumed by grapes becoming wine.
Starlings take to the skies in exquisitely synchronized flight,
spiraling through the twilight like loosed spools of ribbon.

I, too, feel the pull, but there is no possibility of flight. I
am a married woman with children. I have made profound
promises that I intend to keep, but as I watch the starlings
leave me behind, it is not roots that hold me, but the anchor
of a heavy heart. I can't name what is missing, but I am
lonely for it in the violet evening. It is not quite like unre-
quited love; it is more like being in love with nothing at all.

Last week I was standing in the wine aisle of the supermarket staring blankly at the rows of bottles when the grocer asked me if I'd found everything I was looking for. "If
you have any questions," he said, "just ask."

"Do you think that it would be possible for anyone to
find me desirable?" is the only question that came to mind.
It is a phantom feeling, not attached to any known object of

desire. It is I who hope to be desired. *Look at me,* I want to say. *Am I still here?*

When I look into the mirror, I find I have no eyes, no lips, no face. I have to paint in the outlines with firmer brushstrokes and deeper shades each year. Have I completely faded away?

I study the faces of people in the parking lot at Target, the checkout line at Safeway, in restaurants, and at school board meetings. Are they disappearing from their mirrors too? Do they battle the same reckless longings that I do? And if so, how do they stand it? How can any of us stand up straight, carry on, go about our business with the tremendous burden of our losses and our dreams weighing us down?

Later, as I wash dishes, watching out the window as sycamore leaves rain down, scutter across the road, and pile up against the stone fence at the end of the driveway, threatening to extinguish the fire of red roses that have come into extravagant late bloom, I am startled to see my face reflected in the kitchen window above the sink. It is more my mother's than my own. As a girl, I often found her in a dishpan repose, elbow-deep in suds, eyes lost in the unspeakable melancholy of what might have been. I never dreamed that face would belong to me, but here it is staring back from the windowpane.

This year I wrote her obituary. My mother's long life summed up in such a few words. For weeks after writing it, I dreamed of a house on fire, the trees outside it limned in radiant flames, and each night I faced the flames to rescue a picture of her. The photograph in the dream is a real one that came into my possession upon her death. It was taken during the war years when she was in her early thirties. She looks directly into the camera's lens. The expression in her eyes cannot be summed up by telling the world that she enjoyed dancing, fishing, and playing cards, as my father instructed me to write in her death notice.

It hurt to give her life such short shrift and to describe as her own, pleasures I'd long suspected she was only being a good sport about and wouldn't have chosen herself. Why did I play along? I told myself it was what she would have wanted. To make things easier for my dad. She would have condoned my motive, but it felt like a final betrayal nonetheless.

My father's rage at her death was so great that the very day she died, he began purging her memory from his sight. He returned the new outfits she'd bought to wear at Christmas and gave me the store credit. The rest of her possessions —photographs, clothes, shoes, jewelry, makeup, shampoo—he gave or threw away. All the while he sobbed and reminisced about a woman I never knew. The woman she was before she became my mother. The more he talked, the less distinct her memory became to me. *That woman is not my mother,* I wanted to say. He had staked his life on his version of her biography. I could not challenge it even though it meant there was no room for me to grieve the woman I loved. The dream of the house on fire began then.

My mother came of age on a hardscrabble dirt farm during the Depression. She never spoke of it; what I know others have told me. It is my understanding that it was that long-past poverty that caused her to cling to a job she hated for forty years, and drink herself to sleep most nights. When the three of us returned from our annual Florida vacation, she would drink herself into a two-day coma, so much did she hate the idea of returning to that office. When I was old enough to ask why she didn't quit her job, she explained it all in terms of dollars and cents. It was as though no other measure—not peace of mind, and certainly nothing as selfish as her own happiness—could be reasonably factored into the equation.

To understand her surrender, you'd have to have seen the few pathetic Iowa acres where she grew up, the farm that turned to dust the first year of the Depression. My mother's sister told me that she remembered her mother giving birth to the eighth baby on the kitchen table with only her daughters in attendance. "She should have had a doctor," my aunt recalled. "She bled buckets. But the folks didn't have the money." My mother was in that kitchen too. Dad told me that if you've once been hard up, you acquire a healthy respect for your next paycheck, no matter how despised the source. My mother had been hard up.

She worked her way up from switchboard operator to executive secretary in the same firm. She sat behind a boomerang of blond wood outside the boss's office. On her desk were a beige, bubble-case IBM electric typewriter, a Dictaphone with headset, a tan telephone, and an intercom that she called the a-cursed squawk box: "Yes, Mr. Belden. Certainly, Mr. Belden. By 8:00 A.M., sir." She wasn't subservient, exactly. She'd learned, perhaps too well, the lessons of office etiquette taught at business college. It was the same place she learned the trio of skills that sustained her: touch typing, Gregg shorthand, and bookkeeping.

I thought she was beautiful. She had russet hair, the color of autumn leaves, and she wore it in shiny waves swept back into a French twist. She had an emerald-green taffeta dress that rustled glamorously when she danced with my father. I remember watching her, thinking she deserved so much better than the life she lived. She deserved California, where I imagined she would drive to and from the beach in a pink Mustang convertible wearing dark glasses shaped like cat eyes, a pink chiffon scarf wrapped around her hair, trailing in the breeze scented by Tigress perfume.

There was a good reason why the stage set for these daydreams was always California. She had lived there for a few years while my dad was overseas with the navy during World War II. She talked about it for the rest of her life in the same wistful way one would describe a first love. I believe it was that for her. She hated the Minnesota winters and loved the camellias and magnolias and azaleas that turn even February in California into a false spring. It was lush, she would say.

It would have suited her, a California garden of night-blooming jasmine, gardenias, and fairy-tale jacaranda trees in improbable purple bloom. The lush life. If my father ever understood that that was what she wanted, he pretended not to. She fell asleep in the big chair every night, a highball beside her, Johnny Carson on TV. If I came home with a friend, I would go in first and whisper to her, "It's time to go to bed, Mom."

Perhaps it was watching my mother anesthetize herself, trying to quench a bigger thirst, slake her heart's desire, that made me such a restless girl. As soon as I could drive, I would take the burgundy Mustang on aimless, urgent rides down country lanes, looking for an escape route along roads that all dead-ended in cornfields.

She'd told me many times the story of the trip that took her from California back to Minnesota. She remembered stopping every fifteen or twenty miles to patch a flat and blessing every slow leak and puncture in those war-weary tires for delaying the inevitable. Whenever they started rolling, the speedometer "ticked off the miles like a time bomb," she said. "Boy, did I cry." I think she realized she was headed for a life sentence of making the best of and settling for less. In my wanderings along gravel roads, I was looking for a way out for both of us.

Duty was the reason my dad gave for having to return to Minnesota. He had to go back to take care of his mother and father, who had fallen on hard times and needed help to save their farm. For Mom it must have rung too true, like a death knell. Farms had proved to be such bad luck.

She never fit in with his family. They are a fault-finding, humorless tribe, good church people who somehow missed the sermons on Christian compassion. My aunt once introduced my mother to someone by saying, "This is my sister-in-law; she's nothing." She belonged to no church, is what the aunt meant, but it was a shock, and because my mother was incapable of outrage, especially in defense of herself, it was a wound. What is the defense against such people? She forgave; she sought to excuse their behavior as one would overlook a physical infirmity. "It's not her fault, dear; she was born that way." She made the best of it.

She was stuck with dreams of eternal spring in a life that offered nearly nonstop winter. Life, to her, was a wish in the constant hope of being fulfilled: Imagined sable was nearly as warm as the real thing; movie star romances more fun at a glittering distance; and her appetite for lobster dinners, most often remembered and very rarely indulged. Yet she was never thwarted or bitter. She held on for dear life to the philosophy that you never knew what might happen next. Until the end, at age eighty-six, she played the scratch-offs, the lottery, slot machines, hoping to win the jackpot and be set for life. Death ended the suspense.

I am forty-two, and I miss my mother every day. I had not reckoned on her death. No matter that her health was frail and her age great. I had not predicted how completely she would leave this world. My aunt—the dreaded sister-in-law—turned to me the day after her death and said, "This is going to spoil Christmas." For once she was right. Death spoils everything. Dead is over; dead is gone; dead is done. It is the absolute end of desire and luck. It is the end of shy hope. No more lottery jackpot. No more chance of it.

After my aunt's remark, I stopped talking about my mother and professed only sadness, when in fact I had set about the task of making a hallowed place within my heart for her to live. I became fiercely determined that mere words would not diminish the memory of her life as they had the thing itself.

My father refused any acknowledgment of her remains. He said he'd seen too many men die in the war to believe that there was anything left of a person after death. There was no funeral or memorial. He would not choose a receptacle for her ashes or look at the one I chose. It fell to me to be the lone pallbearer. A eulogist sworn to silence. I put her ashes in the trunk of our car and brought them home to California.

All these long months later, after even the most well-meaning friend assumes I've mothballed my mother's death like winter woolens, my dreams are filled with wildfire, and, awake, I am at a loss, a sailor marooned on an uncharted island in an ocean tossed by waves of wishful thinking and treacherous whirlpools of longing. All the things that will never be crowd up around the things that must be, leaving me with the sensation of falling in love with birds on the wing, with beguiling skies. The trembling, rushing after I know not what. The pull toward something familiar but not known. Then, all at once, I have a name for it: It is her hunger I feel, not my own. In holding her so close to my heart, I made her misery mine.

When the birds rise up now, their number is so great that they cast a shadow like the gloom of a gathering storm. My mother and father walk hand in hand, silhouetted against this solemn light. She leaves him, turns, and comes toward me. I am overjoyed to see her. I can feel the warmth of her touch, see the tenderness in her eyes, and I am transfixed by the hope of holding on to her and the sure knowledge that I cannot. Death is the curse of mankind. A lonely migration we must make one at a time.

At this kitchen window, in a feeble moonlight, while black cats stretch on the porch railing, I am at last lost to grief. I weep for my mother's secret dreams. And for myself. For all of us. I grieve for our lonely hearts, unknowable, or perhaps only unknown, unmet. I wring my hands. I pace and fret, fearing despair will be the end of me. I sob into a dish towel; then, spent, I sit down to write, not a eulogy, but a plea, a prayer for the grace to say good-bye. I am a married woman with children. I must make the best of a bad thing and carry on.

It is near the end of the starling season. Before long they will rise up as one and briefly put out the sun. Then they will be gone. The sky, empty and blue. In no time at all, the mock orange will fill the air with its intoxicating scent, and the camellias will come into bloom. To me, the reality of their dreamy beauty is no sweeter than the wish of it. I never told my mother that when I had the chance, and I'm glad of it. It was the promise of flowers in February that sustained her in the face of stubborn fate, just as it is the hope of heaven that comforts me now.

THE EARLY LAND

JANE BROX

We call the small rocky field across from the farmhouse "the early land." It usually dries out by the first or second week in April, and for as long as I can remember, it had been the first field my father worked every year. Always the same. One morning I'd hear the tractor engine, even and deep, as he made his way across the winter rye, leaving a wake of polished, turned-over soil. The spring air steepened with the smell of mineral earth, and the work year all of a sudden felt open to me—all we look forward to, all we're responsible for, our clear and narrow way.

Not that the work hadn't started months before. By this far into the year, the apple and peach trees have been pruned and their cuttings lie in windrows, waiting to be gathered into brush piles. And in the greenhouse, fragrant with damp peaty growing mix, tomato and pepper seedlings are warming in trays. But pruning and greenhouse work begins while the world is still spare and cold. The footprints we make in soft noonday mud are frozen in place the next morning. To me, it doesn't seem as if the spring really starts until I hear the tractor turning over that first field.

How different the same sound can feel at different times. The mourning dove's first solitary call of the year one bright spring morning isn't the same as her call extinguishing the August dusk. And the cut of a relic scythe used rarely and self-consciously—how can it sound the same as a scythe used as an everyday tool?

My father died in late December. Now, my brother alone works the tractor across the rye, and I'm apprehensive when I hear the reliable sound of its engine. I can't help but wonder about what's to come, and how all of us will get along. I wonder if we've learned what we need to keep things going. My father knew so much about the land, the crops, the weather, a knowledge grown into over the long years of his life, a knowledge we'd come to depend on.

All winter, with the snow, the quiet, the fire I'd looked into for months, I was afraid of how the spring would make me feel. I was afraid I'd miss my father most when the season opened up again. But now that I'm out picking up the prunings in the orchard and gathering them into piles of brush, walking back and forth among the rows of spare, turned trees, I'm starting to feel more sure of my responsibilities. He'd say work was good for that, for getting out of a doubting winter mind.

As I trace the way my father worked for countless seasons, I can't help but think about the course of his life. As he carried the farm through this dark, accelerating century, it couldn't have been easy. He had to make his own lone decisions as he faced the passings of the ones he himself loved and relied on. The very sounds of his work changed relentlessly. Before the entrenched noise of a tractor in the fields, he knew only the patient breathing of oxen and workhorses.

I always think of my father on his tractor—that's what I remember—but he liked to remember how he plowed the early land with a matched pair of horses. Back then he must have felt some of the apprehension I feel now as he stepped into the soft, turned earth, certain of nothing other than the love he had for this place.

FISSURES IN THE MOON

SHARING PAIN IN ORDER TO HEAL

GLORIA WADE-GAYLES

As a young girl, I loved the night. During the summer especially, I loved the night. The sun would set, darkness would descend, and within seconds there would be light in the sky above and light in the world below, my world of childhood games and fantasies. In the very instant that moons and stars appeared, the light in the middle of the courtyard would come on with a brightness that beckoned my friends and me from our apartments to play games more exciting and mischievous than those of day. I would lean my head against the lamppost and, with eyes closed, count down to zero as my playmates took cover behind cars and bushes that were perfect hideaways only at night. I loved lying on my back and, with my friends, playing imaginary games with the lighted darkness above. As the daughter of a woman who loved the heavens, I often pretended that the moon was following me—from the courtyard to the ice cream parlor up the hill, then down the street and around the corner from my unit— and that the bottom star in the Big Dipper was blinking a message just for me.

But even when it was not summer, I loved the night, for only then was the city alive from the street up with motion and color. Again, Mama comes to the center of my memories. She, my sister and I, and our stepfather would go for rides in an old Ford to see the magic of neon signs. As we approached Crump Boulevard, a long thoroughfare of businesses and restaurants whose lighted signs made up for the absence of a skyline in Memphis, I could see a large blue pigeon flapping its wings up fast. On and off the lights went; up and down the wings moved. I loved the lighted bird but not as much as I loved the lighted woman. A tourist attraction befitting the Old South, she was black. She was large. She wore a red bandanna and a white apron. The rolling pin in her large hands moved back and forth. On and off the lights went, rolling the pin back and forth.

As an adult woman, I have loved the soothing/stroking gift of night. In the solitude night can bring, I have space and time for meditation, relaxing baths, reading, writing, and knitting fancies with the threads of my imagination. Perhaps my love for the night explains why Langston Hughes's poem about night coming on tenderly "just like me" was easily one of my favorites from his early period. Night always came on tenderly for me, with magic for me, with excitement for me, with a feeling good about what I had completed with the end of day.

Now night comes on menacingly. I rush home to be inside with blinds drawn, doors locked, and my ears deaf to the ringing of my bell when night falls. I need not look through my windows to the world lighted by nature and by man to know that stars are missing from constellations I once knew by shape, location, and name, and that a fissure has crossed the circumference of the moon. I am terrified of the night.

Who was he, I want to know. When and why did he decide to steal the night from me? Did he plan the theft for weeks, days, hours, or only for a second? Where was I, what was I doing, what was I wearing when he decided to remove the pane from a downstairs window and enter my space unseen and unheard? Why did he choose *me*?

Perhaps I did not draw the blinds when I danced in my bedroom. Perhaps I played Aretha and Patti so loudly, their sensuous voices wafted from my den to the world outside. Perhaps I wore too heavy a scent of my fragrance in the grocery line or smiled too warmly when he cut in front of me at a traffic light. Perhaps I took the lighted darkness for granted and, as punishment, I lost the night. I whip myself.

The sting of my whip is most severe when I remember the repairman who came after I had called a company the book said was bonded. A strong wind had pulled the front door loose from its hinges. It would not lock. It had to be repaired. I watched as his large hands removed the door, shaved it smooth at the top, and returned it to hinges that fit perfectly. I remember showing him the rocking chair I had purchased for Mama six months before her death, which later became an heirloom I wanted to pass on to my children and thereafter to their children. One of the posts had pulled loose from the top. I asked if he could fix it. I knew that he could. He was a carpenter who worked with fallen tree stumps, carving them into art pieces that would sell for a good price at an art fair or an Africentric homecoming. He had brought several pieces with him for my purchasing. A carpenter. A black male carpenter. I hired him to fix my mother's rocking chair.

On the day he was to return, I arranged for two of my students to be present; one of them, Chabwera, large-boned and straight from the steel mill world of Gary, Indiana, to pose as the son who lived with me. We played well the game we had rehearsed before his arrival. I fussed about the mess in my son's room. My son fussed back at me. He was supposed to be tough, rebellious, a man doing his own thing, but a son who loved his mother. Our staged argument ended in an embrace.

When I revisit that night, I revisit that scene, and the carpenter's eyes I had thought twinkling and kind become glassy and menacing, floating in something that changed him from artist to would-be rapist. I whip myself.

But I do not know it was he who stole the night from me. The voice was not his, but then, it was disguised, and the face . . . It was flattened beneath a stocking cap made from women's nylons, and I saw it in one quick flash before he covered my eyes. In my sane moments, coming more frequently with the passing of time, I know that it could have been anyone crazed enough, drugged enough, and woman-hating enough to attempt rape. I did not dance the fissure into the moon. It had been there night after night for all women.

I have taught this truth for decades, but always in what I know now to be the hollow voice of an academic standing at a safe distance above a deep well describing for those standing with me the designs desperate fingers have made on the walls, measuring the steep drop that makes climbing out alone an impossibility, and counting the number of bruised bodies I never touched.

I have wept over the accounts of my sister ancestors raped by white men, and with each tear I scream out in rage: "For this, I will never forgive them. *Never!*" I know now that consummate rage cannot comprehend the magnitude of that violation.

I have been incensed by Eldridge Cleaver's confession (or is it braggadocio?) in *Soul on Ice* that he practiced raping black women in order to perfect the technique he would use when raping white women, the prized victim, but I was not incensed enough.

I have attempted to keep some semblance of order in polemics around Cholly's rape of Pecola in *The Bluest Eye* by underscoring the context in which the violation occurred and celebrating Toni Morrison's genius in writing sensitivity into so horrible an experience, but I think now about putting Cholly's pain aside and gouging out the blue eyes that haunted all the Breedloves, all black people in fiction and in reality, in order to writhe in pain for poor, poor Pecola.

I have asked students to critique Susan Brownmiller's *Against Our Will,* a needed and brilliant study, for its dismissal of the race factor, but I know now that the book's weakness is not a racial cataract through which Brownmiller saw the horror, but rather her inability, which was mine as well, to present the horror of the horror.

I had been enlightened for decades, but ignorant, unknowing, untouched by the horror of rape that removes the epidermis and takes the breath away. Now I preface every discussion of rape with "We cannot know its horror unless we hear the voice that says, 'If you scream, I'll kill you.'"

I have honored black women all of my life for their wisdom, their resilience, their integrity, the many strengths which make me weep with pain and dance in celebration each time I read Du Bois's "On the Damnation of Women." Some small thing I, too, would do "to their memory." I know now, however, that the black women I should have honored most were black women who remained sane after being raped. Had the stranger succeeded in the rape attempt, I would have lost my mind.

I share my experiences with my students in order to heal myself, yes, but mainly to add a human voice to this horror which has not been studied enough. I begin by reinforcing what they already know: that you should always listen to your mind, to that small voice that tells you "Do this" or "Don't do that." I didn't listen. On the night that stole the night, I was simply too exhausted to listen. I had spent the day cleaning and shopping in preparation for a visit from my aunt in utter celebration of the joy we would experience during her three weeks with me, our first extended time together, just the two of us, since Mama's death. I had worked late into the night on my writing, because I had no intention of touching it during my aunt's visit. I wanted to savor fully every second we spent together.

At one-thirty I turned off the computer, making certain to save a chapter for a book that would later become *Pushed Back to Strength*. I would be surprised if I had not talked to the document or to the computer, or to both as I have been known to do. "Now, don't forget me. I'll be back in a month with more memories." I turned off the computer and the light and plopped, literally plopped, in bed, falling in an exhausted state on my stomach. I remember trying to roll over on my back because that is how the chiropractor said I should sleep in order to end the back pains which, thanks to my following those orders, ceased five years ago. I remember hearing an inside voice: "Get up, Gloria, and lock the bedroom door."

I answered, lying on my stomach, too tired to roll over, "I'm okay. I'll be safe. The alarm system is on. I'm okay. Really, I'm okay. . . ." Who needs sleeping pills or wine or nature tapes when you can fall asleep in the middle of a being-safe sentence?

Some pieces of the night are racing around in my subconscious so fast, I cannot catch them. Bit by bit, with the passing of time, they stand still long enough for me to catch them, and then I remember what for months I could not remember, or did not want to remember. But with a vividness that remains mysterious, three years later, I never forgot being awakened by my inside voice: "Gloria, you have a crazy imagination. You think you are one of the victims in *Jagged Edge.*" I was so intrigued by the tightly woven mystery of the film that I watched it twice in search of early clues about the identity of the rapist who murdered with a jagged knife. I should have been too frightened by the horror of rape to watch it through a first viewing. I wasn't, and perhaps that is why the night happened.

I remember feeling that my hands were tied and a jagged-edged knife was pressed against my throat. "My god but media is some powerful," my inside voice said.

I heard a voice that was not mine: "If you scream, I'll cut your throat." The flattened face in *Jagged Edge* never spoke. I shifted in my sleep. It was then I felt the body and the knife and knew from the pulling that my wrists were tied. I screamed an inhuman sound. It was . . . it was a gurgling sound, a guttural sound, the sound of a moan in a deep cavern, the sound of breath being sucked from the body. I screamed from a place that has no air, no light, no shape, no dimensions. I screamed from the very abyss of terror. I screamed in a way that only those in consummate dread can scream and only those in consummate dread can hear.

"Oh, so you're gonna be like that?" he said, pulling the rope and pressing the knife against my throat to let me know that it was real, metal and jagged. He taunted me, calling me names I remember and sometimes do not remember. He would kill me. Then. That very second because I was "like that."

The voice that came from the abyss pleaded with him. "Don't kill me. Please don't kill me." Had I ever told students that's what rape victims say? That they plead for their lives? That they are deferential to those who hold them down? That they say "please" and "sir." Did I tell them that pleading is as humiliating as the rape attempt is frightening? I could not have told them any of this because then I knew only the statistics of rape, which are cold and therefore have no human pulse, no sweaty palms, no shortness of breath or lack of breath, no voice pleading for life. I now see a new horror in the horror African women experienced on slave ships that rode the waters that moaned. They could not scream, could not plead for mercy, in a language their violators understood. To scream, to know that you are heard, is the only right the violator has not taken from you.

Cooperate. He asked me to cooperate with his violation of me, and I called him "sir." I wanted to tell him that I am a good woman, that I love our people, that I do volunteer service, that I don't male-bash, that I understand what a hard time "they" have. But *he* wasn't the victim. I was, and to save my life, I sought to cooperate. Three years hence, I hate the sound of the voice that awakens me in nightmares: "Please don't kill me. I'll cooperate, sir. Just don't kill me. Please." I don't remember that line in books about rape.

His orders were simple. I was to roll over on my back.

But the how of my rolling over was not simple. From my right to my left, he insisted. He demanded. The opposite direction would have posed a problem for him. He had to keep his hands on the rope which kept my wrists tied. "From right to left," he shouted. In a weak voice that shames me still and probably will shame me for the rest of my days, I promised to roll over as he ordered—from my right to my left. As I concentrated to follow his orders, I kept thinking of all the people I had called "friend." Surely they could feel me reaching toward them. Surely someone I loved knew I was in danger, knew I was alone in my small bedroom with a maniac whose weight each second became so heavy I thought my back would break into tiny pieces. I did not cry. I could not cry because I was concentrating on which side of my body was right and which was left. Confused, I made an effort to roll over (how I do hate myself), but in the wrong direction. His rage was sharper than the jagged-edged knife. The breath went out of me again, so sure I was that he would kill me and rape my lifeless body.

He screamed the directions again, and I answered, "Sir, I'm trying. I'm trying." I was, but something prevented me from remembering my right from my left and prevented him from carrying out his threat to kill me "right now. I can do it right now."

Details run from me.

I remember being dragged from the bed to the floor and landing, miraculously, on my stomach with him again on my back. In the dragging, I remember catching a quick look at his flattened face. I would not look again during the horror.

I remember my face being pressed into the rug and covered with a towel.

"Where your money?" he asked, making his weight heavier.

I wondered again why someone, anyone, somebody, anybody, whom I had befriended or whom I loved, did not know I was in danger. How does this happen? I kept asking myself. And how do you fight for your life when you are on your back and your wrists are tied . . . ? Where had I gone wrong? What god had I angered? Why hadn't I locked my bedroom door? Why hadn't I listened to myself? Why was this happening to *me*? To *ME*!

I was deferential again. I called him "sir" and told him where he could find my money, my purse, encouraging him, pleading with him, to take all of it. A second time I angered him. I had no money.

"Two goddamn dollars." He repeated the phrase several times, his anger rising. Two dollars because I had recently returned from a summer workshop at New York University. Two dollars because I was spending from traveler's checks. Two dollars because I had been so busy writing and cleaning and preparing for the celebration with my aunt that I had not taken time to go to the bank. Two dollars.

But how did he know I had only two dollars? The realization that he had been inside my apartment, searching through my world before he bounded onto my back pulled from the abyss that inhuman sound I had made when the horror began.

I lied to him. I had more money downstairs. Where? He had checked already. It's in a secret place, I told him, that has a code. What's the code, he wanted to know. I began calling out numbers, but he interrupted me. "If you're lying, I'll cut your throat."

Did anyone ever say you shouldn't lie to a rapist? Would I tell my students not to lie to a rapist? Had I ever read that victims, held down, lose everything, their sense of taste and touch, their knowledge of right from left, their breath, their respect for the truth when a lie can cost them their lives?

I screamed more hysterically than ever, begging the "sir" for my life because two dollars in cash was in fact all the money I had. But I had a bank ATM card, and if he would just untie my hands and let me up, he could follow me, it's right around the corner, I would drive, I would never look at him, I would never tell, I could get the money, cash, I would give it to him, I would not look at him and I would never tell.

Details run from me.

I do not know how I survived disappointing him, angering him, a second time. I remember hearing him give me a third order: "Where your jewelry?" Everything I owned in the way of jewelry was in the middle drawer in the dresser directly behind us. But it was Africentric jewelry purchased from the Shrine of the Black Madonna, a local black cultural center, where the glitter of silver earrings and bangles is reflected in the glossy covers of books about our ancestors, black women and black men, brought to these shores, their wrists tied, their ankles shackled, women's bodies raped with impunity; or at ethnic fairs where sisters and brothers in naturals of various lengths or in locks entice you to their wares with the smell of incense; or in the Spelman courtyard on a Friday afternoon where community vendors wearing their locks and burning their incense are lost in a crowd of Africanity; or at downtown Macy's where a large table of discounted jewelry might contain something for a woman who celebrates being of African descent.

He raised himself up from my back just enough to reach behind him, pull out the drawer, and dump everything inside onto the floor. I could hear him rummaging through the Africentric jewelry—all of it inexpensive and many of the earrings missing a mate. Before he spoke, I could feel his rage rising, for there was nothing in my cache of jewelry he could sell hot on the streets or to pawnbrokers. The experience gave me a new reading on pawnshops that own busy corners in the black community. The people who own and run those shops are accomplices to crimes. They do not care that someone had been brutalized before the ring, the television, the watch, the hot item was stolen. They give mere pennies for heirlooms of inestimable value and sell them beyond our ability to rebuy. They violate in the bright of day and with sanction.

Only now do I think about pawnbrokers. On the night when the stranger stole the night from me, I thought only of how to stay alive. Not how to prevent the rape, but how to stay alive. Did we ever say that some women choose between the two? I feared for my life, not simply my body, because three times I had disappointed the stranger. I couldn't roll over right. I had only two dollars in cash. And I had no gold chains. Three strikes. I lost my breath again in the scream that came from the place where there was no air, no light, no promise of life.

Did he hit me? Did he pull the rope more tightly? Did he press the knife again? What did he say to me? I cannot catch the details. All I know, all I remember, is that a voice inside told me to extend my left hand. I obeyed. With incredible calmness, I said, "Here." It was an unpretentious but beautiful ring with a cluster of tiny diamonds. A ring my mother purchased from one of my Chicago uncles. A ring with an interesting heirloom story I would pass on to my children along with the rocking chair, the photo albums, songs and stories from my youth, my people's legacy of struggle, achievement, and humanity. The ring Mama was wearing on the day of her death. The ring the chaplain had placed into the palm of my hand when he said, "I'm sorry." The ring I had not removed from my finger in six years.

He studied the ring. I knew he was studying the ring because he was both silent and still. I began to breathe again and to think, to reason, for the first time since the horror began. I began to think about someone other than myself. I thought about my daughter and I wanted to live, had to live, in order to tell her that this really happens. That women are powerless if the violator comes while we are asleep. That guns won't save us, neither will knives or Mace or black-belt karate skills. That you make inhuman sounds of dread. That you call him "sir." That you cease to breathe. That he loathes you. Loathes you for breathing, for being a woman. That it is his loathing of you that ties the wrist, presses the knife, and would enter you in order to tear you not to feel you. I *had* to live in order to help my daughter understand the horror and, by some miracle, avoid it.

The ring pleased him. He had something for his troubles, and now he could rape me. I felt him raise himself slightly, unbuckle his belt, and unzip his pants. He did not scream at me as he had in his first order. Instead he spoke in a low voice, strange in its calmness: "Open your legs." He was going to sodomize me. I did not panic, for something happened to me while he studied the ring. The silence was generative and transforming and maternal. My mother's ring. My maternal concern for my daughter. And the invoking of my son's name with a suddenness and a courage that surely came from a place where miracles are born.

"I will not!" I screamed at him. He kneed my legs, and they were pulled tightly together by a force other than my own. He tried to jam them apart again. I felt pain, not fear.

"I will not cooperate with you." I did not call him "sir." Did he hit me? The details run again, but I hear my courage. "Do whatever you are going to do. I don't care. Kill me if you want to. I don't care because I am dying anyway. I have AIDS." I offered my weight as proof, suggesting that if he didn't believe me, he could check my closet and see clothes for a woman larger than I.

I was no longer a woman about to be raped and killed, or killed and then raped. I had become a woman who was the daughter of a mother, the mother of a daughter, and, with the sound of a passing car, the mother of a son. Where did the words come from, I wonder? I spoke them with such certainty: "You don't have time to rape me. That's my son coming home from work."

"Shut up."

With calm. "He will kill you. You don't have time to rape me, and you might not have time to save your own life."

He jerked me from the floor, shoved me into the closet, put the writing table up against the door, and left with these words: "You'd better not move. I'll be back. Goddamnit. I'll be back."

How many minutes passed in the dark closet I do not know. I cannot catch the details, but I remember knowing that I was safe, knowing that he had satisfied himself with more than an hour of loathing and with the treasure of my mother's ring. I pushed hard against the door, removing the writing table inches enough for me to squeeze from the closet. Quickly I ran to the bedroom door, locked it, and made a call to my son who was in Atlanta for the weekend visiting friends. The hour was 4 A.M. He never gave me a chance to tell him I had survived the physical rape. He heard the words "Jonathan, someone" and began screaming immediately. "No," he screamed again and again, the wound coming from a place he had never before known.

Sometimes it is his scream, not mine, that I hear in my nightmares, and, when I awake, it is my daughter's arms, not mine, that remind me how wonderful it is to be alive. A hundred times I have replayed the tape of my rush to the airport two days later to meet the plane that carried her from graduate school home to Atlanta in order to comfort me, to be with me, to see with her own eyes the absence of visible scars and to hear with her own ears my promise that I would be okay. In time, I would heal.

My son's friends, members of a high school group called the Cru and members of Kemet, an African fraternity, came one by one to comfort me and to pledge themselves as African American men to do what they could to end the madness. They never asked for details. I was alive, sitting among them, forcing my lips into smiles. They were comforted, but greatly saddened. That a black man had attempted to rape their "mother" weighted them with anger and with guilt. They volunteered, one by one, to live with me, knowing that Jonathan would have to return to graduate school in

South Carolina. Forever if I needed them. They called, one by one, every night and every morning to check on me and on Jonathan who, for a week, sat awake throughout the night, sitting in Mama's rocking chair facing the window from which the intruder had skillfully peeled away the rubber bindings, removing the entire window to prevent the tripping of the alarm. His father and I never bought him guns when he was a child, but my son, at twenty-three, for more than a week held a loaded shotgun with mastery.

What I learned from my experience is the dread decent young black men have of rape—that each time it brutalizes their mothers, their sisters, and their sweethearts, it etches them in national thinking as criminals who should be avoided, who should be feared. The intruder stole the night from me, the beauty of lighted darkness, and from these young men and others like them, he stole their right to be respected as decent men and their ability to prevent the pain their sisters suffer. Their tears for me and other black women were mixed with tears for their gender/race as well.

I learned also that Jonathan was blessed among the group. I had been spared the brutal entering. The mother of a friend had not. Never should we judge. Never. I had judged the young man for not sticking it out with a project he had begun in Washington, D.C. When the going got tough, I thought, he came home. Just pulled up stakes in D.C. and came home. Only after my trauma with the attempted rape did I learn that he gave up his dream in D.C. in order to comfort his mother after the horror of a rape. Never should we judge. I had always loved this friend of my son's. Now I love him even more.

My daughter's friends talked less about the attempted rape than the young men, and I understood their reticence. After all, women live daily with the fear of rape or attempted rape, and perhaps more than a few of them had experienced "date rape." Then, too, my son and my daughter responded differently to their sharing of the horror with their friends. Jonathan, in a fit of rage, gathered his friends for my protection and for a very heavy sermon, I learned much later, about the need for men to speak out, to effect change. Monica, immersed in fear, kept her friends at arm's length from the horror, protecting my privacy and preventing herself from plunging into hysteria. As a result, what little her friends knew came not from her but from others tapped into the Atlanta University Center grapevine. Their eyes asked questions they did not dare ask Monica and certainly not me: "How did it happen?" "How did you survive?" "Do you hate men?" One eye-question in particular caused me concern: "Are you telling the truth? Did he really leave without raping you?" The pendulum of interpretations would swing on any day of the week from "He raped her" to "He didn't rape her," the former supported by the certainty that I am too proud to admit to total victimization and the latter by my visibility at all the events I am required to attend.

He didn't rape me physically, but he raped me spiritually. Did I ever discuss rape and attempted rape in my women's studies classes? When rejecting the Western concept of duality of soul and body, did I ever think about the difference between rape of the body and rape of the soul? Are they different? Of course they are. The women who are raped, and always brutally because rape is always brutal, are far more victimized than I, but there is a point on the continuum of horror where together we cling to life. Once in the hands of a rapist who binds your hands and presses the knife against your neck, who presses the weight of his body against your own, you are raped. Did we ever talk about that in my classes?

Once we had gasped at the statistics of rape, did we discuss the aftershocks which, for me, were often as terrifying as the incident itself and more than a few times more terrifying? In one, he raped me. In another, he cut my throat before raping me. In still another, he cut my throat after raping me. In yet another, he stood over me, with eyes bulging from the flattened face. Should I tell my students the gory details? Is that tasteless? I struggle with how much of the horror I should share with them. Always I struggle, wanting to teach, to enlighten, to remove the ignorance without robbing them of the night.

Do I tell them about the many women who have sought me out to tell me about their own horror? One by one they came within weeks after the incident, some of them strangers, others I have known for years. Some had been raped by strangers and others by "dates," two of whom were men of standing and status in the black community. I found myself a member of an unbelievably large group which included women of various ages, body sizes, complexions, and professions. None had worn a too-short outfit, none had said "no" teasingly, none had invited the rape, and only one had told. As a colleague in North Carolina told me two years later in a discussion of violence against women, "Rape is such a common experience for women that in the course of one year in graduate school, every *one* [her emphasis] of my women friends had been raped. Black women, Latina women, Asian women, white women."

Do I tell my students about the unexpected pain created by women you had considered friends, sisters, sister-daughters, spiritual kin? Given the bonding you have with them, you expect the most comforting embrace from these women, but in some cases it does not come. They know about your horror, and yet they say nothing. In their silence, you feel the pressure of a different knife. "If they cared . . . ," I found myself saying, but perhaps their caring is so deep, they do not know how to express it. Do not judge, I tell myself. Do not judge harshly.

My nightmares are not as terrifying or as frequent as they once were. Talking has helped, but there are yet times when I lose my breath at the thought of someone expressing sympathy or asking questions. Sometimes I do not admit even to myself that I was almost a victim of rape.

Meditation has helped.

Reading has helped.

Stretching toward more spirituality has helped.

And even a bit of levity has helped—that is, when I am in one of my talking-to-heal-and-to-inform moods. Levity? No chance, you say? Needed, I say, to keep my listeners from jumping out of their very skins when the horror has a human voice.

"Listen, be prepared. Whatever you do, don't go to bed without money. Having only two dollars almost cost me my life. So make sure you have cash, on hand, for the would-be rapist. Leave it on the dresser with a note."

Laughter. Nervous.

"If you play music before you go to bed, whatever you do, don't, I repeat, DON'T play Aretha or Patti. Play . . . [pause for effect]. Play 'Amazing Grace' or something like that."

Nervous laughter.

"How many of you have gold chains? I mean real gold chains?" No hands. *"Well, buy you one. Buy you one good-looking real gold chain, and before you go to bed, leave it on the dresser for the would-be rapist. With a note."*

Laughter.

It's real. Women know it is real. One by one, women said, "I live with that nightmare."

I never did. I didn't think I was immune or undesirable (because it's not about desire; it's about consummate loathing). I just never thought about it, never let it enter my world of possibility or probability, never feared it. Perhaps that is why it almost happened to me. I was too academic in my approach to rape and too arrogant, or vain, in my ownership of the night. I danced for myself in the moon that followed me, never stopping to see fissures that shattered the night for hundreds of thousands of women.

There is a side of me that is grateful for the theft because it has bonded me with every woman who walks the face of the earth; because it has given me consummate respect for, humbling me in the presence of, women who remained sane and functioning after being physically raped; and because it has prevented me from pretending to know, even intellectually, that about which, even with the facts, I am ignorant. I will never again attempt to speak for any group of which I am not a bona fide member. Something is lost in the translation.

I heard the news that "he" had been caught. Friends called: "Watch the six o'clock news," they said. I turned on the television. Monica said, "Mom, don't watch. Don't watch." I put my hands over my eyes as I listened to the anchor reading the teletape about attacks on women in a West End neighborhood. Monica did not trust me *not* to look. She stood in front of the small screen, and she said again, "Mom, don't watch." How strange to have his face inches away from mine and not see it. I wanted him to see mine in the full light of day, to see my body sitting tall on a sofa, fully dressed and protected by my daughter's love. I wanted him to see the face that asked the question "Why?" and the question that, even today, I am ashamed to have asked: "Why me?" How odd I felt hearing the nightmare of hours reduced to a ten-second sound bite!

The neighbor who knew the carpenter called: "It wasn't him," he said. Relief! A day later, uncertainty. He was not the intruder, but knowing how to enter my space, perhaps he had drawn the map. Like battered women, victims of rape or attempted rape drink an acid mixture of pain and guilt.

Most nights I can sleep with the lights off, a great loss to the utilities company, and most nights I have no nightmares. I am healing. I can stand in a grocery line without putting a flattened face on every man I see and idle at a traffic light without fearing that when the light turns green, he will follow me. I no longer scream when someone touches me on the shoulder in the bright of day, and I no longer badger my daughter with a hundred and one tips on how not to be a victim of rape, all of which at one time seemed to recommend withdrawing from life. I am better, much better. Healed, not fully recovered. But I am saddened by the realization that, for years, I have deluded myself into believing I am a pacifist, a woman opposed to war and to any deliberate act of violence. I now know that I *can* kill. Any man who attempted to rape my daughter, I *would* kill. With my bare hands, I would kill.

QUERIDA NURIA

JOAN LINDGREN

Querida Nuria,

I write to you after our visit to tell you that although I cannot precisely see your face in my mind, I cannot forget it. Everything about your appearance, in fact, seemed to me to be faintly speckled—your eyes, whose green cannot stay put but keeps fusing into the hazel; your hair, an aura more than a mane, black but dappled with last year's henna, and strewn with fine gray wires. You kept running your delicate hands through its airy density. Your skin, a fragile skin flecked with sun and perhaps the first spots of old age. It may be because I had read your book before I met you that I take away with me the impression of a skin burned and then healed, though there is no actual scarring.

Of course I had to read your book before meeting you, and of course it would affect my impressions of you. How do people who have not read of your years as a political prisoner, tortured and starved in a concentration camp—how do they see you upon meeting you? Simply as a small, delicate-boned, pretty woman dressed with an inexpensive but innate elegance?

So slim you are that I kept thinking of a pencil, worn with the work of its life, half or more of its years cruelly shaved away. You wrote the book, you said, because you had to, and published it knowing it needed work, but knowing also that it needed to be read as is, before the patina of time might soften its impact.

But more vividly the image of a bird prevails. You fluttered about that office distracted, waiting, wondering what to do with me, a visitor from your daughter's city, a translator, a writer. The work of your United Nations–funded office is to receive phone calls from desperate women, to offer calming words and advice, a hot line, we call it. Later, traitorously—and I understand this because I am a translator-traitor—the despair of the callers is processed as data, and the causes of female depression are charted and printed and distributed to social institutions. You, who have been caged and tormented, the toy of torturers, have now—to earn a living—to be an agent of the helplessness of women at large, who, try as they will, cannot break the chains of hegemony: cannot please their lovers, cannot overcome their need for the plasma of consumer goods, cannot open for their children the doors barred to them by the political and social reality of Chile today.

Those poor dusty trash-strewn miles I traveled by taxi through the city to reach you revealed rows of shop windows filled with cheap imported goods that are to compensate the Chilean people for the hemorrhage of Chilean fruit, picked at starvation wage. And Chilean minerals mined in the most dangerous and unhealthy work known to our species for the proverbial pittance.

Nuria, I want to take back every word I spoke to you that day. I want only to bask in the truth that hung unspoken in the air about us. That in the years when your children had to be sent into exile abroad while their mother languished in Grimaldi or Los Alamos, my children were safe and sound in San Diego, California, and blessed with an unquestioned future. By our government, of course, democratic and humane at home, yet engaged in Chile in the machinery of destroying the people's government of your country. I cannot stroll the streets of your city in innocence—every well-dressed woman appears before me with pot and spoon in hand,* every well-dressed man of my age is the pawn or collaborator of Pinochet.

When at last your office captivity came to an end, you took me home with you. Peñalolén, Alta Peñalolén, the place where you live far removed in the outskirts of Santiago, is your refuge. I was enchanted. There in the fields dotted with fruit trees, a hand-built house with its floor and chimney of stone, tree trunks for support, everywhere slabs of wood, varnished and polished. And the windows, tall and narrow like Chile itself, inviting the landscape to remain beautiful, at bay. Not a single excess in that house. A rocking chair with a crocheted pillow, and the tablecloth also your handiwork, but no curtains against the outside.

We made the tour of the grounds and you didn't need to tell me how you had planted each and every tree. Horses pawed and whinnied in the next field over, where a caretaker lived with his family, one of those residual families of the *campo* who had squatted there, a *paracaidista,* or parachutist, they are called; one of his children, sleek and black-haired, came to you softly, reverently, with a message. That child had a passport to your universe that I lacked. You touched his hair.

Then you cooked us a fish lunch, and we sat over wine and spoke of our mothers—mine, victim of other political strife, other abuses; yours, bereft, stunned, when in your early years your father committed suicide. Both intense, energetic, creative women—self-willed and let-down. You carried on the tradition better than I—how, after all, be at sword's point with, free yourself from, a mother so used by

---

* Shortages and hoarding, often manipulated by influences outside the Allende government, had the effect of dividing the Chilean people. The image of a middle-class housewife, spoon and pot in hand to be used as a drum of protest, helped to undermine solidarity.

the system? And from great distances your daughters adore you.

In the bedroom I looked in and saw posters of Matisse nudes above the altar of the bed. Your husband, of the same Grimaldi history, had stopped in at the office earlier. He kissed you, and you couldn't know that the angle at which I stood allowed me to see how your tongues interlaced. Under the crocheted coverlet there must lie consolation; there must be where you remind one another that life is ongoing. I felt surprise, and joy, for you. And I knew you were waiting for his return as much as for my own departure.

You were a perfect hostess, polite and considerate to the letter, and I don't know if it was just a bad day for you—you sleep badly, perhaps?—or if every day that a woman from my country comes to visit is a bad day for you. But I felt you could hardly wait to be done with me. I didn't take it personally, but I knew the kind of optimism, enthusiasm for changing the world that runs in my Yankee veins exhausts you. It did not, does not serve you. I left you there in your beautiful house, a small bird still, made rare by circumstances in a cage of her choice.

Strange. The kind of solidarity you envisioned for your people was a pole of your life. Now the other pole claims you—isolation, privacy, the security and comfort and self-expression of the *hogar*, home, the castle of the body as the body is the castle of the self.

I want to thank you, Nuria, for you taught me about silence, though I did not exercise it, though I learned in reflection, not on the spot. But I could sit there with you now in silence, if need be forever, in the tranquil loveliness of Peñalolén, the great *cordillera* visible through the small-paned windows—the only place in my days in Santiago where this wonder of Chile was in fact to be seen. The late afternoon birds at their bedtime ritual, the grapes languorously dripping from the arbor, the cuckoo clock insistent. I could breathe it all in now in silence, knowing better there is a time for silence. You showed me what the poet Roberto Juarroz had told me: that in the mind's eye we draw windows to see through in this life without exit, not doors. That the business of life—to learn how to die—is beautiful beyond all witnessing there in Peñalolén. That in the shadow of Chile's great *cordillera,* among the fruit trees and the caretaker's brown-skinned, spark-eyed children at the business of being children, there is a quiet, costly grace.

Gracias.

MOODSWINGS AND MIDLIFE

NEARLY GETTING TO NIRVANA

ELAYNE CLIFT

In the beginning there was bliss: long, languid, delicious mornings reading in my sun-filled bedroom, absolute quiet surrounding me with the gorgeous sound of stillness; nature walks; coffee and the paper in local cafés; deep conversations with my best friend in California. And only the slightest, occasional moments of angst. I didn't worry about these uncomfortable little intrusions until I noticed that my wee lie-ins were extending to midmorning and that I was feeling ever so slightly reclusive and depressed. When I began to have fantasies of becoming either a rabbi or an emergency room nurse in order to imagine a meaningful future, I knew I was in crisis and called the coast.

"I really think I'm going crazy."

"Been there," my best friend said. "Didn't like it."

She'd just been fired and had come through a messy divorce, whereas I had slid, not altogether voluntarily, from increasingly part-time work to quasi-retirement.

We spend a lot of time, my friend and I, processing our depression, anxiety, and panic attacks as we contemplate how, as positive and powerful women, we are going to live the final third of our lives. I articulate my need for meaning, creativity, and connectedness. She tells me that's why she loves me. When I tell her I am feeling spiritually hungry, she confesses she has started Hebrew lessons so that she can be Bat Mitzvah when she turns sixty. Through all the years of our friendship, we have validated each other in this way through rough waters, bruised psyches, and the jungles of modern life and mean workplaces. Ours is a rare and wonderful relationship, and without her, I doubt I'd have made it this far intact.

Here are some of the things I've shared with her:

First, it has hit me that, despite my years of activism on behalf of the world's women, I'm never going to be on Gloria Steinem's Rolodex. Bella Abzug is not going to ask for my help, and Betty Friedan is, in all likelihood, not inclined to quote me. Staunch feminist that I am, I must come to grips with the fact that, at best, in the world of feisty feminists, I'm second string. This is very painful because I live in a city where power and prestige are everything, and while I don't necessarily aspire to high-stakes political positioning, I can't bear feeling marginal either. I would like to feel that I'm still part of the action. At the same time, I want out. This odd dichotomy must be somewhat like being involved in a dysfunctional or abusive relationship. The activist agenda is my seducer, even though I know that once it has its way with me, I will inevitably get hurt. On the other hand, my transcendent self wants to move to a higher plane, to leave behind the banalities of the working life in order to get in touch with my spiritual essence, to live a life of meaning. Much of my lie-in time is consumed with this dilemma.

I contemplate the wholesale marketing of postmenopausal zest (PMZ) during my transcontinental phone calls. This trend is, generally speaking, a good thing. For too long before this movement began, menopause was considered a disorder if not a fatal disease, and older women were written off as just so much degendered detritus. My concern is that the wholesale selling of a zestful second half assumes that I haven't been living that way in the first place, and that has a way of riddling me with a kind of nondescript guilt when I strive for the high road. My personal theory is that PMZ plays well to women who have been liberated from limited adult lives, whatever form these may have taken. But I, for one, am tired. Worn out, actually, by running to catch up in my thirties and forties. Exhausted by starting organizations, fighting political battles, creeping my way to a graduate degree, juggling multiple roles, struggling to keep a sagging spirit intact. I no longer have the requisite energy to get very excited about too many issues anymore. I'd actually like the second half (or the final third) to be anything but a mindbender. I'd like it to be easy, comfortable, and ever so slightly self-indulgent. So why is a good Jewish girl like me burdened with such an insatiable Protestant ethic embedded in my brain?

Along these lines, there's the issue of aging. All the hype about PMZ notwithstanding, I can't altogether buy into the power surge package. Yes, it's liberating to be postfifty, but let's face it, there's also the firm-to-flab phenomenon, not to mention fatigue and the fatalism of our inevitable demise. I wonder all too often where my muscle tone, my stamina, and my libido have gone. In short, aging gives me the blahs big-time. I get irritated by Lauren Hutton's radio commercials in which she coos, "I love my age! I wouldn't go back to being twenty-one for anything!" This from a woman who has never borne, birthed, schlepped, or nursed babies and who spends God knows how many hours a day with a personal trainer? Please!

But the larger issue, as I search for midlife balance, tranquillity, and purpose, has to do with meaning and where one finds it.

When I was in my twenties, it seems to me, I wanted to know the meaning of life. In my thirties, I quested for meaningful work. By the time I entered my forties, I was satisfied if I could simply figure out what things meant (in the cosmic sense, of course). But now that I've entered my fifties—the ultimate "mean" if not median—I find I'm oddly disinterested in much of what usually imbues a certain kind of activity with meaning. I'm increasingly de-invested. Lazy, perhaps. At any rate, I no longer seem driven. If I died tomorrow, I figure, I'd still have a pretty impressive obituary.

At the same time, because this seeming ennui is rather out of character for me, it has become a source of psychic conflict. My present struggle, if written as an equation, might look something like this:

$$A = \frac{P - M}{ML}$$

or, Angst = Personality minus Motivation over Modern Life.

One of my problems is that I continually feel like I've "been there, done that," and there's a weird sort of déjà vu quality to most events; my life seems to keep repeating itself. I long for something truly original to occur, for some *aha!* experience, for new nuance. Instead, I am beginning to feel like people do when they say, "Y'know, if you live long enough, all faces start to look the same." Sometimes I think this is nothing more than the winter blues or the summer doldrums. But no variation in temperature, humidity, or daylight seems to affect my lingering malaise.

There is an upside to this, of course. It's great not to be so driven or crazed with the quest for achievement. I like the fact that I'm finally learning the art of laid-back living. I really do smell the roses differently these days. But a little bit of motivation in moderation wouldn't hurt either.

So . . . am I having a mild moodswing, a true midlife crisis, a great growth spurt, or am I simply poised to plunge into the depths of despair? Perhaps I've stumbled onto something—the Great Transition, that spiritual awakening that comes of soulful solitude. Or maybe I just need a new cause, a new town. . . .

While I make light here of my struggle for passage, my quest for renewed identity and newfound energy at midlife (plus) is really no laughing matter. I have had deep moments of pain and confusion, isolation and fear, as I experience the birth of a redirected Self. Had I tried to write this piece before my most recent soul-cleansing California call, it might have read quite differently and been a solemn affair. But right now—this minute—having understood that I am not alone and that my quest is not such a unique thing after all, I can lighten up, take my time, see the options as a gift. It is not always so. Sometimes, in place of those options, there is a terrifying void looming thirty years large ahead. When those dark moments seem more than I can possibly sort out, I try to remind myself that I am in the best of company. It is indeed a good thing, needing the creativity, the meaning, the connection to a wider world, and we women who seek it are not the crazies. We are, rather, the caretakers of souls— our own, and very often those of the people we love. It is good to examine our past lives now and again, to discard what is moldy and faded, to air the treasures in which there is still life, to add a few new pieces to our traveling repertoire. Deep down, I know this. Just as I know I will find myself, at least for a time, in new and comfortable terrain.

Of course, no matter where I end up, there will always be a direct line to California. And at the end of the day, that, perhaps, is the most comforting thought of all.

UNDER THE THUMB

HOW I BECAME A POET

MARGARET ATWOOD

I recently read an account of a study that intends to show how writers of a certain age—my age, roughly—attempt to "seize control" of the stories of their own lives by deviously concocting their own biographies. However, it's a feature of our times that if you write a work of fiction, everyone assumes that the people and events in it are disguised biography—but if you write your biography, it's assumed you're lying your head off.

The latter may be true, at any rate of poets: Plato said that poets should be excluded from the ideal republic because they are such liars. I am a poet, and I affirm that that is true. About no subject are poets tempted to lie so much as about their own lives; I know one of them who has floated at least five versions of his autobiography, none of them real. I, of course, am a much more truthful person than that. But since poets lie, how can you believe me?

Here, then, is the official version:

I was once a snub-nosed blonde. My name was Betty. I had a perky personality and was a cheerleader for the college football team. My favorite color was pink. Then I became a poet. My hair darkened overnight, my nose lengthened, I gave up football for the cello, my real name disappeared and was replaced by one that had a chance of being taken seriously, and my clothes changed color in the closet, all by themselves, from pink to black. I stopped humming the songs from *Oklahoma!* and began quoting Kierkegaard. And not only that—all of my high-heeled shoes lost their heels and were magically transformed into sandals. Needless to say, my many boyfriends took one look at this and ran screaming from the scene as if their toenails were on fire. New ones replaced them: They all had beards.

Believe it or not, there is an element of truth in this story. It's the bit about the name, which was not Betty but something equally nonpoetic, and with the same number of letters. It's also the bit about the boyfriends. But meanwhile, here is the real truth.

I became a poet at sixteen. I did not intend to do it. It was not my fault.

Allow me to set the scene for you. The year was 1956. Elvis Presley had just appeared on *The Ed Sullivan Show,* from the waist up. At school dances, which were held in the gymnasium and smelled like armpits, the dance with the most charisma was rock 'n' roll. The approved shoes were saddle shoes and white bucks, and the evening gowns were strapless, if you could manage it; they had crinolined skirts that made you look like half a cabbage with a little radish head. Girls were forbidden to wear jeans to school, except on football days, when they sat on the hill to watch and it was feared that the boys would be able to see up their dresses unless they wore pants. TV dinners had just been invented.

None of this—you might think, and rightly so—was conducive to the production of poetry. If someone had told me a year previously that I would suddenly turn into a poet, I would have giggled. (I had a passable giggle, then.) Yet this is what did happen.

I was in my fourth year of high school. The high school was in Toronto, which in the year 1956 was still known as Toronto the Good because of its puritanical liquor laws. It had a population of 650,509 people at the time and was a synonym for bland propriety, and although it has produced a steady stream of chartered accountants and one cabinet minister, no other poets have ever emerged from it, before or since—or none that I know of.

The day I became a poet was a sunny day of no particular ominousness. I was walking across the football field, not because I was sports-minded or had plans to smoke a cigarette beyond the field house—the only other reason for going there—but because this was my normal way home from school. I was scuttling along in my usual furtive way, suspecting no ill, when a large invisible thumb descended from the sky and pressed down on the top of my head. A poem formed. It was quite a gloomy poem; the poems of the young usually are. It was a gift, this poem—a gift from an anonymous donor, and, as such, both exciting and sinister at the same time.

I suspect this is why all poets begin writing poetry, only they don't want to admit it, so they make up explanations that are either more rational or more romantic. But this is the true explanation, and I defy anyone to disprove it.

The poem I composed on that eventful day, although entirely without merit or even promise, did have some features. It rhymed and scanned, because we had been taught rhyming and scansion at school. It resembled the poetry of Lord Byron and Edgar Allan Poe, with a little Shelley and Keats thrown in. The fact is that at the time I became a poet, I had read very few poems written after the year 1900. I knew nothing of modernism or free verse. These were not the only things I knew nothing of. I had no idea, for instance, that I was about to step into a whole set of preconceptions and social roles that had to do with what poets were like and how they should behave. I didn't know yet that black was compulsory. All of that was in the future. When I was sixteen, it was simple. Poetry existed; therefore it could be written. And nobody had told me—yet—the many, many reasons why it could not be written by me.

At first glance, there was little in my background to account for the descent of the large thumb of poetry onto the top of my head. But let me try to account for my own poetic genesis.

I was born on November 18, 1939, in the Ottawa General Hospital, two and a half months after the beginning of the Second World War. Being born at the beginning of a war gave me a substratum of anxiety and dread to draw on, which is useful to a poet. It also meant that I was malnourished. This is why I am short. If it hadn't been for food rationing, I would have been six feet tall.

I saw my first balloon in 1946, one that had been saved from before the war. It was inflated for me as a treat when I had the mumps on my sixth birthday, and it broke immediately. This was a major influence on my later work.

As for my birth month, a detail of much interest to poets, obsessed as they are with symbolic systems of all kinds: I was not pleased, during my childhood, to have been born in November. November was a drab, dark, and wet month, lacking even snow; its only noteworthy festival was Remembrance Day, the Canadian holiday honoring the war dead. But in adult life I discovered that November was, astrologically speaking, the month of sex, death, and regeneration, and that November 1 was the Day of the Dead. It still wouldn't have been much good for birthday parties, but it was just fine for poetry, which tends to revolve a good deal around sex and death, with regeneration optional.

Six months after I was born, I was taken in a wooden box to a remote cabin in northwestern Quebec, where my father was doing research as a forest entomologist. I should add here that my parents were unusual for their time. Both of them liked to be as far away from civilization as possible, my mother because she hated housework and tea parties, my father because he liked chopping wood. They also weren't much interested in what the sociologists would call rigid sex-role stereotyping. This was beneficial to me in later life, as it helped me to get a job at summer camp teaching small boys to start fires.

My childhood was divided between the forest, in the warmer parts of the year, and various cities, in the colder parts. I was thus able to develop the rudiments of the double personality so necessary for a poet. I also learned to read early—I was lucky enough to have a mother who read out loud, but she couldn't be doing it all the time, and you had to amuse yourself with something or other when it rained. I became a reading addict and have remained so ever since. "You'll ruin your eyes," I was told when caught at my secret vice under the covers with a flashlight. I did so and would do it again. Like cigarette addicts who will smoke mattress stuffing if all else fails, I will read anything. As a child I read a good many things I shouldn't have, but this also is useful for poetry.

As the critic Northrop Frye has said, we learn poetry through the seat of our pants, by being bounced up and down to nursery rhymes as a child. Poetry is essentially oral and is close to song; rhythm precedes meaning. My first experiences with poetry were Mother Goose, which contains some of the most surrealistic poems in the English language, and whatever singing commercials could be picked up on the radio, such as *You'll wonder where the yellow went / When you brush your teeth with Pepsodent!*

Also surreal. *What yellow?* I wondered. Thus began my tooth fetish.

I created my first book of poetry at the age of five. To begin with, I made the book itself, cutting the pages out of scribbler paper and sewing them together in what I did not know was the traditional signature fashion. Then I copied into the book all the poems I could remember, and when there were some blank pages left at the end, I added a few of my own to complete it. This book was an entirely satisfying art object for me, so satisfying that I felt I had nothing more to say in that direction and gave up writing poetry altogether for another eleven years.

My English teacher from 1955, run to ground by some documentary crew trying to explain my life, said that in her class I had shown no particular promise. This was true. Until the descent of the giant thumb, I showed no particular promise. I also showed no particular promise for some time afterward, but I did not know this. A lot of being a poet consists of willed ignorance. If you woke up from your trance and realized the nature of the life-threatening and dignity-destroying precipice you were walking along, you would switch into actuarial sciences immediately.

If I had not been ignorant in this particular way, I would not have announced to an assortment of my high school female friends, in the cafeteria one brown-bag lunchtime, that I was going to be a writer. I said "writer," not "poet"; I did have some common sense. But my announcement was certainly a conversation stopper. Sticks of celery were suspended in midcrunch, peanut butter sandwiches paused halfway between table and mouth; nobody said a word. One of those present reminded me of this incident recently—I had repressed it—and said she had been simply astounded. "Why?" I said. "Because I wanted to be a writer?"

"No," she said. "Because you had the guts to say it out loud."

But I was not conscious of having guts, or even of needing them. We obsessed folks, in our youth, are oblivious to the effects of our obsessions; only later do we develop enough cunning to conceal them, or at least to avoid mentioning them at parties. The one good thing to be said about announcing myself as a writer in the colonial Canadian '50s was that nobody told me I couldn't do it because I was a girl. They simply found the entire proposition ridiculous. Writers were dead and English, or else extremely elderly and American; they were not sixteen years old and Canadian. It would have been worse if I'd been a boy, though. Never mind the fact that all the really stirring poems I'd read at that time had been about slaughter, battles, mayhem, sex, and death—poetry was thought of as existing in the pastel female realm, along with embroidery and flower arranging. If I'd been male, I would probably have had to roll around in the mud, in some boring skirmish over whether or not I was a sissy.

I'll skip the embarrassingly bad poems I published in the high school yearbook (had I no shame? Well, actually, no), mentioning only briefly the word of encouragement I received from my wonderful grade twelve English teacher, Miss Bessie Billings: "I can't understand a word of this, dear, so it must be good." I will not go into the dismay of my parents, who worried—with good reason—over how I would support myself. I will pass over my flirtation with journalism as a way of making a living, an idea I dropped when I discovered that in the '50s, unlike now, female journalists always ended up writing the obituaries and the ladies' page, and nothing but.

But how was I to make a living? There was not then a roaring market in poetry. I thought of running away and being a waitress, which I later tried but got very tired and thin; there's nothing like clearing away other people's mushed-up dinners to make you lose your appetite. Finally, I went into English literature at university, having decided in a cynical manner that I could always teach to support my writing habit. Once I got past the Anglo-Saxon, it was fun, although I did suffer a simulated cardiac arrest the first time I encountered T. S. Eliot and realized that not all poems rhymed anymore. "I don't understand a word of this," I thought, "so it must be good."

After a year or two of keeping my head down and trying to pass myself off as a normal person, I made contact with the five other people at my university who were interested in writing, and through them, and some of my teachers, I discovered that there was a whole subterranean wonderland of Canadian writing that was going on just out of general earshot and sight. It was not large: In 1960 you were doing well to sell two hundred copies of a book of poems by a Canadian, and a thousand novels was a best-seller; there were only five literary magazines, which ran on the lifeblood of their editors. But while the literary scene wasn't big, it was very integrated. Once in—that is, once published in a magazine—it was as if you'd been given a Masonic handshake or a key to the Underground Railroad. All of a sudden you were part of a conspiracy. People writing about Canadian poetry at that time spoke a lot about the necessity of creating a Canadian literature. There was a good deal of excitement and the feeling that you were in on the ground floor, so to speak.

So poetry was a vital form, and it quickly acquired a public dimension. Above ground, the bourgeoisie reigned supreme, in their two-piece suits and ties and camel-hair coats and pearl earrings (not all of this worn by the same sex). But at night, the bohemian world came alive in various nooks and crannies of Toronto, sporting black turtlenecks, drinking coffee at little tables with red-checked tablecloths and candles stuck in Chianti bottles, in coffeehouses—well, in the one coffeehouse in town—listening to jazz and folk singing, reading their poems out loud as if they'd never heard it was stupid, and putting swear words into them. For a twenty-year-old, this was intoxicating stuff.

By this time, I had my black wardrobe more or less together and had learned not to say "Well, hi there!" in sprightly tones. I was publishing in little magazines, and shortly thereafter I started to write reviews for them too. I didn't know what I was talking about, but I soon began to find out. Every year for four years, I put together a collection of my poems and submitted it to a publishing house;

every year it was—to my dismay then, to my relief now—rejected. Why was I so eager to be published right away? Like all twenty-one-year-old poets, I thought I would be dead by thirty, and Sylvia Plath had not set a helpful example. For a while there, you were made to feel that, if you were a poet and female, you could not really be serious about it unless you'd made at least one suicide attempt. So I felt I was running out of time.

My poems were still not very good, but by now they showed—how shall I put it?—a sort of twisted and febrile glimmer. In my graduating year, a group of them won the main poetry prize at the university. Madness took hold of me, and with the aid of a friend, and another friend's flatbed press, we printed them. A lot of poets published their own work then; unlike novels, poetry was short and therefore cheap to do. We had to print each poem separately and then disassemble the type, as there were not enough *a*'s for the whole book; the cover was done with a lino block. We printed 250 copies and sold them through bookstores for fifty cents each. They now go in the rare-book trade for $1,800 a pop. Wish I'd kept some.

Three years or so later—after two years at graduate school at the dreaded Harvard University, a year of living in a tiny rooming-house room and working at a market research company, and the massive rejection of my first novel as well as several other poetry collections—I ended up in British Columbia, teaching grammar to engineering students at eight-thirty in the morning in a Quonset hut. It was all right, as none of us were awake. I made them write imitations of Kafka, which I thought might help them in their chosen profession.

I taught in the daytime, ate canned food, did not wash my dishes until all of them were dirty—the biologist in me became very interested in the different varieties of molds that could be grown on leftover Kraft dinner—and stayed up until four in the morning writing. I completed, in that one year, my first officially published book of poems and my first published novel, which I wrote on blank exam booklets, as well as a number of short stories and the beginnings of two other novels, later completed. It was an astonishingly productive year for me. I looked like *The Night of the Living Dead*. Art has its price.

This first book of poems was called *The Circle Game*. I designed the cover myself, using stick-on dots—we were very cost-effective in those days—and to everyone's surprise, especially mine, it won the Governor General's Award, which in Canada then was the big one to win. Literary prizes are a crapshoot, and I was lucky that year. I was back at Harvard by then, mopping up the uncompleted work for my doctorate—I never did finish it—and living with three roommates named Judy, Sue, and Karen. To collect the prize, I had to attend a ceremony at Government House in Ottawa, which meant dressups—and it was obvious to all of us, as we went through the two items in my wardrobe, that I had nothing to wear. Sue lent me her dress and earrings, Judy her shoes, and while I was away, they all incinerated my clunky, rubber-soled Hush Puppies shoes, having decided that these did not go with my new, poetic image.

This was an act of treachery, but they were right. I was now a recognized poet and had a thing or two to live up to. It took me a while to get the hair right, but I have finally settled down with a sort of modified Celtic look, which is about the only thing available to me short of baldness. I no longer feel I'll be dead by thirty; now it's sixty. I suppose these deadlines we set for ourselves are really a way of saying we appreciate time and want to use all of it. I'm still writing, I'm still writing poetry, I still can't explain why, and I'm still running out of time.

Wordsworth was partly right when he said, "Poets in their youth begin in gladness / But thereof comes in the end despondency and madness." Except that sometimes poets skip the gladness and go straight to the despondency. Why is that? Part of it is the conditions under which poets work—giving all, receiving little in return from an age that by and large ignores them. Part of it is cultural expectation: "The lunatic, the lover, and the poet," says Shakespeare, and notice which comes first. My own theory is that poetry is composed with the melancholy side of the brain, and that if you do nothing but, you may find yourself going slowly down a long dark tunnel with no exit. I have avoided this by being ambidextrous: I write novels too.

I go for long periods of time without writing any poems. I don't know why this is: As the Canadian writer Margaret Laurence indicates in *The Diviners,* you don't know why you start, and you also don't know why you stop. But when I do find myself writing poetry again, it always has the surprise of that first unexpected and anonymous gift.

RE-CREATION

SUSAN MARSH

In a recurring dream, I plod through deep snow, away from a small white house. I have left the house for some purpose, but as I pause, afraid to continue, I can't remember what. Panic tugs at my sleeve as I try to make my way back to the lamplit windows before darkness falls. But the snow gets deeper and heavier. Soon my legs will not move. I struggle to pull each foot along, as though walking against a current. The harder I strain, the slower I move, dogged by a vague sense of being pursued, of needing to escape. Panic nudges me awake. In the dark stillness of my bedroom in the middle of the night, I have this revelation: The dream is about my job.

In April, winter softens into spring. The birds return, species by species—robins, blackbirds, geese. The aspens all over Jackson Hole poise to bloom, their pussy-willow globes dropping into long silver tassels. Bursts of rain and snow punctuate the mild afternoon. From my upstairs window I look straight into the branches of an aspen tree, eye level with the birds.

A notebook lies open in my lap to receive a line or two between long periods of watching out the window. I had the dream again last night. Its heaviness remains in my legs and on my mind. I turn in the notebook to a list I made a year ago—of what I sought most from work and life, of where I wanted to be in ten years. The list was my first acknowledgment of restlessness. My chosen profession, to which I have dedicated nearly twenty years of my life, does not satisfy me anymore. Perhaps it never did.

I work in a national forest, where I oversee the management of campgrounds, trails, and backcountry. Government jargon labels me a "staff officer," a title full of power and authority. Or so I thought when I was a college student, working summer jobs at the local ranger's office. Then, a visit from a staff officer was a momentous event. To have him actually talk to me felt as though I had been granted a special favor.

I collected degrees in subjects I thought would get me outdoor work, to reach the heights belonging to those staff officers. A career with the Forest Service sounded like getting paid to walk among the trees. I had only a vague knowledge of the agency and never placed significance on the fact that all the staff officers were men. I knew what forests were and loved them.

Through the years of college, forests lay like mist on my mind. Every morning I stepped from the gray of early morning through the familiar double doors of Haggart Hall. I walked into a cave of bare concrete with moss-green walls, the color of rocks next to a waterfall. I walked past cork boards fluttering with announcements and the giant terrarium where Casey the bull snake lived, into Room 125, for winter quarter chemistry. I registered with satisfaction the scarcity of female faces among the forty students who glanced in my direction. The lack of women told me this was a serious class, not one you passed for merely showing up. "Basket weaving," my fellow students called the courses taken to pad a grade point average or to kill time until someone married you. My load each term was full of meaty courses and labs, most of them held in the basement of that science building. When I left the building at five o'clock, I once again stepped through the double doors, into the gray of dusk.

Now I wish I had taken basket weaving and run my

hands through reed and willow and splints of ash. Weaving strands of wood into useful and beautiful objects would have brought me closer to the forest than biology classes ever did.

My old career goal, long achieved, has lost its luster. I allow the job to eat at me, waking up in the middle of the night to worry about things I cannot influence. I grow impatient with bureaucratic inertia and a conformity that makes anyone who questions it a target. I have been a target instead of the revered staff officer of my fantasies. Even a small reward, a midmorning walk to the ponds north of town to see which birds have arrived, gives only temporary relief from an inexplicable boredom.

How can I be bored with life—abundant, fecund life? A flutter of wings catches my attention as siskins chase each other through the blooming aspen. The birds chirp and skirmish and swell with color. Sunlight pierces the margin of a cloud. Spring rises like a flower ready to burst into bloom. How can I be bored?

I chastise myself, yet I see that the boredom is somehow necessary to my understanding: What once brought me comfort and security has begun to imprison me.

I don't want a job, but a vocation. Creative, life-affirming work. Creativity lives, not at the office, but in flower beds and studios and kitchens, among growing, graceful, and delicious things. It thrives in the hills as they brighten from straw-brown to green, where I watch bluebirds grace the tired fields like fragments of the sky. When I feel guilty for taking a day off to watch bluebirds, I tell myself that when I die, I will not look back and wish I had spent more time at the office. Play is the real work of our lives, recreation. Re-creation.

Out the window, the aspen tree bends against an approaching squall. The notebook closes in my lap. Who am I? Who, of all people, should know better than I? Yet I cannot answer this question. I cannot see myself without a professional disguise. Like the emperor's new clothes, the job in which I cloak myself may be more transparent to others than it is to me.

Who is anyone besides a name, a job, a place in the community? Labels by which we identify each other. I see a face at the bank and make associations: She is a member of the choir, a friend of Joy's with two little girls who go to Coulter School, who lives on Buffalo Drive. The circumstances of a life slowly bring the person into focus, make her recognizable and familiar. But do they tell me who she is? I have defined myself by such circumstances, but they did not tell me who I am.

My friends at work don't wonder who they are. They bustle with activity, planning parties and tending to the affairs of their children. They seem so normal, content and self-possessed, while I wander the halls and glance around my office feeling lost. I search for some deeper meaning of myself, a part that cries to be recognized beneath the order and dailiness. As if life had some meaning beyond that which I give it, as if there were a God with a grand plan for me, as I believed as a child. Perhaps the grand plan is for each of us to find our own true path, by ourselves.

Who I am is no longer what I do. The realization frightens me, since rewards have come only for what I have achieved. I fear what I might find beneath the emperor's clothes. A daydreamer following bluebirds. Staring out the window at aspen trees.

I hear my mother's voice whenever I allow myself the luxury of idleness: *Do something worthwhile. Be productive, don't just sit around.* I conjure her and abandon my contemplation. I must attend to laundry, dirty dishes, errands.

My profession is the small white house in my dream, lit against a snowy night. I step off the porch and walk across the yard, into the dark and silent forest. I turn back toward the light, wondering what prompted me to leave. The hold of the familiar threatens to keep me from discovering the possible.

I realize that I am bored not with life but with myself. Bored with striving, achieving, and guarding my professional self-image. This boredom hits at the time of year when all the world is quickening. A pulse runs through the thawing earth and up the trees, a message whispered ground to branch, picked up by the feet of birds and spread across the sky on their wing beats. Spring is the pulse I want to place my hand on, to hold my ear to the ground and listen for, to dance to.

Perhaps I am acting out my own vernal ritual, like a new leaf pushing off the leathery scale that protected it all winter. I have outgrown a husk that has sheltered me long and well, has given me something to call myself, a place in the world. I am not ready to let it go, not ready to brave the uncertainty that waits. But when I feel the husk around me, I know it is too small.

Ennui. The word haunts me, rattles in the back of my head, appears in my mind uninvited. A feeling of weariness, my dictionary says, arising from lack of interest in the present scene. How well it describes the limbo of change, the vague dissatisfactions of middle age. Slowly my restlessness has filtered into my conscious mind, where it sits like a troll under the bridge, a lump in the mattress. I pace around my office short-tempered. What would fall to pieces if I left?

I need a job; mine is a good one. I run for the lamplit house in the snow. Yet I wonder if I am used up, expendable, in need of replacement. Papers stack up in the in-box I have labeled Do Soon. Every day more of them arrive, and the Do Soon Box becomes a stagnant eddy. I cull it every few weeks and find nothing so urgent after all. What if they replaced me with someone younger and more energetic? She would keep the in-box clean.

Lately I have been drawn to shops that sell perfumes and incense. I buy a bottle of purple ink. I imagine wearing clothes of soft, flowing gauze that drape loosely from my shoulders. My closet bulges with somber gray and blue,

colors that bear witness to longing for acceptance and re-
spectability. When I start wearing gauze, I will follow the
fragrance of perfume wafting out of shop doors. I will relish
the balance in my hand of my pen as it doodles in purple ink.

My office suddenly seems an intolerable mess, with its
stacks of paper and three-ring binders perching on book-
cases. I pull up a chair and a wastebasket and get to work.
Copies of memos I wrote years ago, reports I labored over,
proposals that never bore fruit. A budget report that once
seemed important; I canceled a pack trip to finish it on time.
The pages drop like falling leaves into the trash.

I envy young mothers and retirees who stay at home and
putter in their gardens on weekday mornings in the spring.
Although I am afraid if I were in their places, I would wish
to be back in the buzzing, humming thick of things, productive and needed and busy.

I'm finding that there is no thick of things. We just create a whirlwind of activity for ourselves and spin around in
it until we're tired and dizzy and want to leap off.

I am in the middle of a leap.

One day I stare at my reflection in the bathroom mirror.
Most mornings, I glance at the glass to watch my toothbrush
stirring up a foam but do not really notice who is there. Now
I lean against the sink as if looking into someone else's eyes.
I realize I don't know the person staring back. I know the
one who brushes her teeth and tugs at an earring, ready to
run downstairs and out the door. That familiar face does not
belong to the woman who watches me now. This unknown
person looks strangely serene, calm as a statue. She is a fol-
lower of bluebirds, an idler in the aspens. She is asking me
to introduce myself.

Still staring out the window, I catch a tiny movement
near my face. A spider hangs from the ceiling on a filament
of silk. Her legs are tucked so she looks like a speck of dust,

a gray flake of tree bark. All at once she drops another foot. I catch the strand and lower her to the floor.

What made the spider launch from the safety of the ceiling? She is so tiny, the eight feet to the floor must seem an abyss. But she shows no fear as she rappels from a crag in the paint and drops on her fragile thread. She knows the floor will be there and her landing will be soft. If only I could launch with such fearlessness and grace.

Diane Ackerman is a poet, essayist, and naturalist. Her dozen works of nonfiction include *Deep Play, A Slender Thread,* and *A Natural History of the Senses. I Praise My Destroyer* is her most recent collection of poetry. She also writes nature books for children, the first two of which are *Monk Seal Hideaway* and *Bats: Shadows in the Night.*

A former newsletter editor and longtime resident of Mexico, **Diana Anhalt** is presently working on a book, *A Gathering of Fugitives: Voices of American Political Exile in Mexico, 1948–1965.* Her articles have appeared in, among others, *Grand Tour, Voices of Mexico,* and *Red Diapers: Growing Up in the American Left.*

Joan Arcari states, " 'An Outing with Isabelle' is about my latest transition. I have been a suburban housewife and mother; a single parent, political activist, and feminist organizer; a student and a professor; a passionate traveler and a confirmed city dweller—in approximately that order. My recent novel returns to the suburbs, which is not something I will do."

Margaret Atwood is the author of more than twenty-five books of poetry, fiction, and nonfiction, and her work has been translated into more than thirty languages. Her most recent novel, *Alias Grace,* was published in 1996. She lives in Toronto.

Adrian Blevins is assistant professor of English at Hollins University. She has published poems, stories, and essays in numerous magazines and journals, including *Utne Reader, Mississippi Valley Review,* and *Southern Poetry Review,* with new poems recently appearing in the *Southern Review, Poetry Motel,* and the anthology *We Used to Be Wives.* Her award-winning chapbook of poems, *The Man Who Went Out for Cigarettes* (Bright Hill Press, 1996), appeared in second edition in 1997.

Barbara Brent Brower's poems and stories are regularly published in the Australian journal *Tirra Lirra.* Her poems are included in the Story Line Press anthology *The Muse Strikes Back* and in *GRRR* anthology, published by Actos Press. Her work also appears in journals in the United States and abroad.

Born in Austin, Minnesota, **Margaret Lynn Brown** graduated from the University of Minnesota and worked as a journalist in the Midwest for eight years. After attending a special program for journalists at Stanford University, Brown decided to become a historian. The journey described in this essay culminated in her Ph.D. at the University of Kentucky and her forthcoming book from University Press of Florida, *The Wild East: Creating a Wilderness in the Great Smoky Mountains.*

Jane Brox's *Five Thousand Days Like This One* was published by Beacon Press in 1999. Her first book, *Here and Nowhere Else,* received the L. L. Winship/PEN New England Award. Her work has appeared in *Georgia Review, Orion,* and other periodicals, and is represented in *Best American Essays.* She lives in the Merrimack Valley of Massachusetts.

Kathleen Carr (a pseudonym) resides in Bucks County, Pennsylvania, and teaches at Bucks County Community

College. "Crossing Over" is from a manuscript in progress, *(Re)Constructing Desire: Letters and Works between Friends.* Her long poem *(A)nna (M)orphous: days* sings for its supper, as she works on a philosophical examination of the space of poetics.

Elayne Clift, a writer in Saxtons River, Vermont, teaches at several New England colleges. She contributes to various publications and anthologies internationally. Her latest book is *Croning Tales,* a short fiction collection (OGN Publications, 1996). *To New Jersey, with Love and Apologies,* a coming-of-age collection of prose and poetry, will be published in 1999 by OGN Publications.

Patricia Cumbie's short stories have been published in the *Emrys Journal* and *Hurricane Alice.* She is also an editor of *Lakewinds Natural Foods Cookbook.* She works in the natural foods industry in Minneapolis, where she is a health and wellness newspaper editor. She is currently at work on a novel that examines the nature of ritual in destructive behavior and how such behavior is condoned in our society.

Laura S. Distelheim received her J.D. from Harvard Law School. Her work has appeared or is forthcoming in *An Intricate Weave: Women Write on Girls and Girlhood* (Iris Editions, 1997), *Creative Nonfiction, Whetstone, Jane's Stories II: An Anthology by Midwestern Women* (White Dove Press), *DoubleTake, International Quarterly,* and *Pleiades.* She received a Money for Women/Barbara Deming Memorial Fund grant in 1997 for *Grace Notes,* her collection of literary essays in progress, and the Richard J. Margolis Award in 1998.

K Edgington holds a Ph.D. in literary studies from the American University. She teaches writing and women's studies at Towson University and serves on the editorial board of BrickHouse Press, which publishes The New Poets Series, Chestnut Hills Press, and Stonewall Press. She lives in Baltimore with a feral cat and a broken toaster.

Deborah Fruin is a columnist and copy editor for the *Napa Valley Register,* a daily newspaper in Napa, California. She has worked as a newspaper editor and reporter for the past four years. Before that she worked in the publishing and film industries in Los Angeles and New York. Fruin lives in Calistoga, a small wine country town. She is married and has two sons, Christopher, age ten, and Andrew, age seven.

Diane Glancy is associate professor of Native American literature and creative writing at Macalester College. Her first novel, *Pushing the Bear* (Harcourt Brace, 1996), is about the 1838 Trail of Tears. Her novels *The Only Piece of Furniture in the House* and *Flutie* were published by Moyer Bell (1996, 1998). Glancy, of Cherokee and German/English heritage, received her M.F.A. from the University of Iowa. She has published a drama and numerous collections of short stories, essays, and poetry.

Maria Exposito Glass, Spanish-born writer and teacher, lives in Glendale, Arizona. "The Race" is her fourth personal essay being published in an anthology and belongs to a memoir collection in progress, *No Woman's Land*. She is currently finishing her first novel, *Sun and Shade*, based on events surrounding the Spanish Civil War.

Christine Hale is a writer and teacher. Her articles, essays, and short fiction have appeared in a number of magazines. A 1999 MacDowell Fellow, she is at work on a collection of linked short stories and recently completed a novel, *Basil's Dream*. She lives in Tampa, Florida, with her daughter and son.

Joan Halperin lives in Hastings-on-Hudson, New York. She has two grown children and three grandchildren. Her poems, essays, and short stories have been published in *Rosebud, The Writing Self, Cimarron Review,* and others. She teaches as a poet-in-residence in public schools and in mental health facilities.

Joan Shaddox Isom, coeditor of this anthology, is the author of two poetry collections and a book for young readers, *The First Starry Night.* Her fiction and poetry have appeared in numerous literary magazines and anthologies. A former associate fiction editor of *Nimrod International Journal,* Isom has worked as poet/writer in the Oklahoma schools and taught writing at Northeastern State University (in Oklahoma), where she was assistant professor of English. She holds an M.F.A. from the University of Arkansas.

Beth Kephart is the author of *A Slant of Sun: One Child's Courage* (W. W. Norton), a 1998 National Book Award finalist in nonfiction and recipient of *Salon Magazine*'s Annual Book Award. She also won the 1998 Leeway Grant for nonfiction and was named a 1998 Pew Fellowship on the Arts finalist for the book. Kephart writes reviews and essays for the *Baltimore Sun, Philadelphia Magazine, Parenting Magazine, San Francisco Chronicle,* and other periodicals.

Pulitzer-prize-winning poet **Maxine Kumin** is the author also of several collections of essays; *Women, Animals and Vegetables* is the third and most recent, with a fourth, *Always Beginning* (to contain "Interstices," published here), forthcoming from Copper Canyon Press in the fall of 1999. She has served as consultant in poetry to the Library of Congress and is former poet laureate of the state of New Hampshire.

Tricia Lande's short stories, poetry, and essays have appeared in literary magazines as well as anthologies. She is writer-in-residence at Idyllwild Arts Academy, Idyllwild, California, where she lives with her husband and Dave the Cat.

Madeleine L'Engle has published more than forty books that have won numerous honors, among them *A Wrinkle in Time*, winner of the John Newbery Award, Sequoyah Award, and Lewis Carroll Shelf Award; and *A Swiftly Tilting Planet*, winner of the American Book Award. L'Engle has received special recognition from Smith College, her alma mater, and has been awarded numerous accolades and honorary degrees for her contributions to American literature.

An award-winning short story writer and editor, **Shirley Geok-lin Lim** received the Commonwealth Poetry Prize for her first book of poems, *Crossing the Peninsula*. Her memoir, *Among the White Moon Faces: An Asian American Memoir of Homelands,* appeared in 1996. Her most recent critical study is *Writing South/East Asian in English* (1994). She is a professor of English and women's studies at the University of California, Santa Barbara.

Joan Lindgren is translator and editor of *Unthinkable Tenderness* (University of California Press, Berkeley, 1997), the poetry of Juan Gelman, recipient of his country's National Poetry Prize and voice of the families of Argentina's Disappeared. A frequent visitor to the Southern Cone, Lindgren has widely published essays and translations. Her work with the families of the Disappeared will be documented in a work in progress, *Translating Argentina.*

Mary Anne Maier, coeditor of this anthology, is a Wyoming native. Her work has appeared in such varied settings as National Public Radio, *Journal of the American Medical Association, Christian Science Monitor, Southwest Art,* and *Dutiful*

Daughters (Seal Press). Maier taught college English for several years and more recently served as writer-in-residence at the Oklahoma Arts Institute and presenter at the Poynter Institute's National Writers' Workshop. She is a book editor for Texas Western Press.

Susan Marsh is on the staff of the Bridger-Teton National Forest in Jackson, Wyoming. Her essays have appeared in *Orion, North Dakota Quarterly, Petroglyph,* and *Northern Lights,* as well as other magazines and anthologies. She is currently working on two nonfiction books and several short stories.

Rhonda C. Poynter has been a professional freelancer for twenty years and has written more than seven hundred pieces for magazines, newspapers, and anthologies, including the *Oakland Tribune, San Francisco Chronicle, Chicago Tribune,* and *Comstock Review.* Her new poetry collection, with Warthog Press, is titled *Start the Car.* Poynter has been nominated for five Pushcart Prizes. She states, "My ten-year-old son, Gannon Blue, is mildly autistic and is my grace, my gift, and my one true reason."

Julie Moulds Rybicki is the author of *The Woman with a Cubed Head* (New Issues Poetry Press, 1998). She also served as librettist for the operetta *Baba Yaga, the Russian Witch.* Her journals in this anthology are excerpted from a book in progress about her non-Hodgkin's lymphoma. She lives in Michigan with her husband, John.

A former civil rights activist, **Gloria Wade-Gayles** is author of *Pushed Back to Strength: A Black Woman's Journey Home* and *Rooted Against the Wind,* among others, and editor of two collections. Wade-Gayles's acclaimed teaching within the historically black college system has led to numerous honors and awards. She is a board member of Amistad National Research Center and holds the Rosa Mary Eminent Scholars Chair in Humanities/Fine Arts at Dillard University, New Orleans. She is the mother of two.

ACKNOWLEDGMENT

The editors wish to thank Tisha Hooks of Beacon Press for her sensitivity to our vision of this book.